T0030701

THE GIRLS WHO FOUGHT CRIME

THE UNTOLD TRUE STORY OF THE COUNTRY'S FIRST FEMALE INVESTIGATOR AND CRIME-FIGHTING SQUADS

MAJ. GEN. MARI K. EDER

(U.S. ARMY, RETIRED)

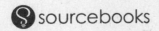

Published by Sourcebooks
P.O. Box 4410, Naperville, Illinois 60567–4410
(630) 961-3900
sourcebooks.com

Library of Congress Cataloging-in-Publication Data

Names: Eder, Mari K., author.
Title: The girls who fought crime : the untold true story of the country's
    first female investigator and her crime fighting squad / Mari K. Eder.
Description: Naperville, Illinois : Sourcebooks, [2023] | Includes
    bibliographical references. | Summary: "From corsets to crime fighting ,
    Mae Foley challenged the patriarchal status quo by not only juggling
    family life, but also by forming the first female auxiliary police force
    in the City That Never Sleeps. After the 19th Amendment passed in 1920,
    Foley galvanized 2,000 women to join her "Masher Squad" and eventually
    became one of the first sworn officers with the NYPD. The "Masher Squad"
    brought down robbers and rapists, investigated the notorious 3X serial
    murders, and provided witness protection during the trails of the
    deadliest mafia bosses in the city. Foley starred down the barrel of the
    gun-from facing the patriarchy head on, but also quite literally-and
    always came out on top"-- Provided by publisher.
Identifiers: LCCN 2022055969 (print) | LCCN 2022055970 (ebook)
Subjects: LCSH: Foley, Mae. | Women detectives--New York (State)--New
    York--Biography. | Women's rights--New York (State)--New York. |
    Women--Employment--New York (State)--New York. | Police--New York
    (State)--New York--History--20th century. | Male domination (Social
    structure)--New York (State)--New York. | New York (N.Y.)--History--20th
    century.
Classification: LCC HV7911.F635 E34 2023 (print) | LCC HV7911.F635
    (ebook) | DDC 363.25092747/1--dc23/eng/20230109
LC record available at https://lccn.loc.gov/2022055969
LC ebook record available at https://lccn.loc.gov/2022055970

Printed and bound in the United States of America.
LSC 10 9 8 7 6 5 4 3 2 1

"Whatever you choose to do, leave tracks, and that means don't do just for yourself, because in the end it's not going to be fully satisfying. I think you will want to leave the world a little better for your having lived."

JUSTICE RUTH BADER GINSBURG

*For the brave women of the New York Police
Department and all those who answer the call to serve
as law enforcement officers, firefighters, and first
responders—past, present, and future*

*And to Mae's legacy of public service: her beloved
grandsons, Bobby and Johnny, and their descendants*

FIDELIS AD MORTEM

CONTENTS

INTRODUCTION

I stepped into the massive packing box of an elevator with the tick of the closing door ratcheting my heart rate up a notch. At first, there was a heady mix of the import of the moment and a hint of excitement. It was the first time I'd been to One World Trade Center, on yet another clear September day, now nearly twenty years since 9/11 and the attack on the twin towers. The second tick came from just a hint of fear. I'm not a fan of high-rise elevators, and the ride from the ground floor up to One World Observatory promised to be fast and dizzying.

It took just forty-seven seconds to shoot up to the 102nd floor. The building is a symbolic 1776 feet high and 104 stories in total. Even so, the ride was enthralling, and I didn't even have a moment to think about the high-rise ride. I was too absorbed in the incredible story unfolding in front of me.

The video walls of the elevator tell the full story of the growth of New York City in those forty-seven seconds, graphically playing out the city's rise out of the earth along the river to seeing buildings rise higher and higher,

tighter, and closer. Traffic increases from horses to motorcycles and automobiles, then cars, buses, and a million honking taxis, while planes appear,
become increasingly sophisticated, and begin marking the sky with crossing
white lines of their trails. I turned around and around. Trying hard not to
blink, I held my breath as years flew by in mere seconds. The twin towers
came and went. Then ding. The doors opened and the intoxicating expanse of
New York in all its glory—past, present, and future—was laid out in front of
us. In every brilliant direction, there lay history, a million stories, and a future
to behold.

The spirit of New York is the story of America—immigration, industry,
invention, crime, punishment, education, development, and pride. All those
human endeavors that made the years fly by in forty-seven seconds.

Mary "Mae" Vermell Foley lived through perhaps just a brief flash of that
fast film drama playing out on the elevator's walls. She was the daughter of
immigrants, born on the cusp of the twentieth century, her life story a part
of the quintessential dynamic of New York and America itself. It was still
Victorian times when Mae came of age. Women wore long skirts and carried
parasols on the streets. They couldn't even vote yet. But Mae knew what she
wanted; making a difference was part of her plan.

She was barely out of high school when she began to work for the city.
Soon she found herself juggling husband and kids while she fought to form the
first female auxiliary police force in New York City, galvanizing two thousand
women to join her reserves. After the Nineteenth Amendment was ratified in
1920, Mae continued to challenge the patriarchal status quo, becoming one of
the first sworn officers with the New York Police Department (NYPD) and
working a variety of assignments that ranged far afield from her beginnings
in social welfare.

Arriving on the force from a background in social work and limited experience as a volunteer in the Women's Police Reserve, she was among the first to join the force as a young wife and mother. Once a sworn officer, Mae served first with the newly minted "Masher Squad." There, she brought down robbers and would-be rapists, then became a detective, investigating the notorious 3X murders, and provided witness protection during the trials of two of the deadliest Mafia bosses in the city. She faced down criminals with guns more often than not and always came out on top.

Before and during World War II, she worked undercover, infiltrating the American Nazi movement in New York. She also investigated potential acts of enemy espionage and sabotage across the city. Her skills in investigation, detection, and jujitsu made her the perfect crime fighter, close-mouthed intelligence officer, and dedicated public servant.

Through her decades of service with the NYPD, she experienced the full impact of the major events of her time—not merely as a witness to history but as a participant, right at the center of the action. And woven throughout her twentieth-century experiences, she lived her police officer's oath—the need to protect the vulnerable and innocent juxtaposed against the concurrent growth of crime and the burgeoning presence of law enforcement. The NYPD needed talented women more than they knew. The vulnerable and the victims needed female officers too. The criminal element perhaps didn't need policewomen digging into their business, but once that happened, they quickly learned to respect what women brought to law enforcement. The three *i*'s were inseparable—insight, investigative ability, and instinct. Mae and her cohort of female officers had those talents in abundance. Succeeding generations would rely on them as well, sometimes covertly or as a background skill, but always with strategic purpose. They got results.

Policewoman Mae Foley in 1935. Uniforms had just been issued
to women on the force. Her purse held a slot for her police .38
revolver and her lipstick. (Photo courtesy of the Foley family.)

Her friends were Broadway stars and playwrights, judges, and politicians. Film star Rita Hayworth often babysat for her young grandsons. She saved up for her infrequent vacations and used them to transport herself into another world. She loved to travel, living the dream in first class on many an international cruise, and found her way around the world more than once. From riding camels to dodging communist customs agents, Mae was always up for adventure and a good time.

She was a policewoman, a detective, a crime solver, a meticulous investigator, a wife, and a mother. Widowed at a young age, she raised two daughters while working long hours in shift work, nights, and weekends. She did it all at a time when that "having it all" fullness of experience just wasn't done, much less even considered an option. She never considered she couldn't have what she wanted, be what she wanted. She just decided she would. And she did.

And she'd play it all off, even well into retirement. At age seventy-four, "Queens' most famous 'Pistol Packing Mama'" was modest about her career achievements. "Ah, I was a bit of a tough egg in those days," she'd say, waving a hand. "I knew how to handle a gun."[1]

But finding the details of her story as well as those of her contemporaries and peers wasn't easy. There is little written about women in the NYPD in the early twentieth century, and records are difficult to locate, if they exist at all. In a New York Public Library blog article, Andy McCarthy commented, "For the five boroughs, there really is no collection of historical 'police records.'" He suggests that prior to 1930, "any smattering that was kept and saved resembles a hail of rocks launched from a Bowery window during the 1857 Dead Rabbits Riot."[2]

While this obscure reference seemed odd to me, I quickly learned the facts. There are no NYPD personnel records prior to 1930. What little information exists is available in fits and starts, indeed scattered across the city's various libraries and other records holdings areas. The department doesn't have a historian. It doesn't provide access to its historical photos. The New York City Police Museum closed in 2019. It was time to look elsewhere for resources and support.

I found numerous books, articles, and blogs on law enforcement typically included only mere snippets of facts or brief references about women's contributions to policing. Many barely mentioned the women who served. Some citations omitted the female officers altogether, focusing instead on major crimes, show trials, and the personalities of criminals and politicians. But for fresh insights, there are the newspapers of the day. With all their faults, inaccuracies, politics, attitudes, and gossipy opinions, they still provide incredible insight into the life and times of Mae Foley, her cohort of fellow policewomen, her contemporaries, and all those who followed in their footsteps.

Those times evolved in New York and her NYPD throughout the twentieth century, in the technology and application of police science if not in culture. By the time Mae retired in 1945, women comprised about 12 percent of the NYPD. Across the country, this was an average statistic.

Typical stereotypes about women in male-dominated industries continue, refusing to let go—particularly in the realm of traditionally macho professions such as the military and law enforcement. According to a recent article in *Police Chief* magazine, while the research confirms not only the need but the benefit of more women in policing, the numbers are not increasing. "This may be due to an unwelcoming culture within many police organizations," the article states. Ongoing stereotypes "create formidable barriers for female applicants and women navigating the profession."[3]

By 2019, the number of women serving in the NYPD had increased to only about 18 percent, about 6,570 women in the 36,500-member force. They included 781 detectives, 753 sergeants, and 200 lieutenants.[4] One of those detectives had moved on to serve as the chief of detectives in Nassau County, New York. In 2022, she returned to New York's finest.

On January 1, 2022, Keechant Sewell made history when she was sworn in as the city's forty-fifth police commissioner and the first woman to hold the post. In an interview after her appointment, Commissioner Sewell said, "I grew up in Queens. This is my city, and now this being my department, I feel like I've come full circle."[5]

The Girls Who Fought Crime takes us back to the beginning of these linked circles. This is Mae Foley's journey, a tale that takes us from the age of corsets to crime fighting and the love of a city that she knew could never sleep. This is the chronicle of one courageous woman's legendary dedication to public service and her fight to find a way into service that matters.

I was advised against writing this story. "No one wants to read about police these days," I heard. Like so many things in America these days, the topic of policing has become politicized and polemicized. However, the stories of our first policewomen are important for the exact reasons I was being told they weren't worth telling. Policewomen have been shown to help decrease violence and the abuse of power that so many now associate with the sight of an officer with a badge and gun.

So we can't turn away from our policewomen, especially now. A number of police departments are calling for more women to serve, seeing their involvement as "integral to reducing police misconduct, and the use of force."[6] Perhaps this harkens back to Mae's time and the policewoman's original tie to the notion of social work extending into law enforcement, serving for the public good, truly to protect and defend. A 2021 study by researchers from four universities found that "female officers made 7 percent fewer arrests than their male counterparts while using force 28 percent less often."[7]

Just like in Mae's time, the data shows us that female officers are typically more educated than their male counterparts, more likely to engender a perception of fairness and equal treatment in their communities, and more likely to express empathy and engage with victims and suspects both as people first.

Thus, this is the quintessential American tale, not a tragedy but a drama, full of hopes and dreams, fights and dirty politics, scandal and violent crime. This is a story of women taking control back from powerful men and using it for not just their own good but the good of those around them, for their communities and society. But it is also a story of how one woman succeeded despite the odds at a time when success wasn't only considered impossible but when those who applied and tried were often scorned. She not only saw it all; she did it all and fully understood why and how she was needed. Like many of her trailblazing contemporaries, she did it at a time when her ambition and courage made her stand out. Her lessons are fresh for us today.

CHAPTER 1
BORN LUCKY, GROWING UP TOUGH

"I just need to check you now for any weapons. Stand here with your arms outstretched. I'm going to pat you down. It will only take a moment."

"You bitch!"

Detective Mae Foley thought she'd seen it all in her twenty-seven long years with New York City's finest. Then, when she least expected it, one loud and volatile woman who'd just been arrested turned on her, right there in the station house, and proceeded to kick, punch, and headbutt like a prizefighter defending her title belt. Mae needed to examine the prisoner, make certain she wasn't hiding a weapon. But with an unholy shriek, the woman turned into a real contender and proceeded to pummel Mae with everything she had.

Taken by surprise, Mae hit back, but even with all her skill, strength, and training, she took some serious blows in the process. After she won the fight, in a mere three rounds by her count, Mae limped into the ladies' lounge, sucked in a deep breath, and took stock in the mirror: bruised ribs, maybe broken, a black eye, throbbing head, skinned knees and knuckles. Right then, she knew it was time to make the big decision.[1]

She looked in the mirror and told herself, "Enough is enough. And at fifty-seven, you aren't getting any younger." Of course once she said that, she still had to wonder if she would actually listen.

By the fall of 1945, she'd lived an incredible and exciting career but a dangerous one too. She was a minority—a woman in a typically male role, a career police officer, a detective, an undercover agent, and sometimes a spy. All those roles at a time when any one of them would be considered unconventional in society. She was also a wife, mother, widow, grandmother, and world traveler. Mae found her way in the world and blazed her own trail. She never looked back. Now, she had a choice to make. She tried to wink at herself in the mirror, but her swollen eyes wouldn't cooperate.

Mae spent a few days at home, nursing her injuries and her wounded pride, but she already knew what she had to do next. While brutal, this most recent incident that led Mae to make the big decision to turn in her badge wasn't the first time she had had a run-in with a prisoner who turned violent. Throughout her career she'd been shot at, held up, beaten, even used as bait. Mae was tough. More than once, she caught herself thinking that she was done for, but she always came through.

Born on July 14, 1886, to French and Irish parents Robert and Mary Ann Vermell, Mae was baptized just days later at the Immaculate Conception Church, her parents and neighbor and now godmother Mrs. Bridget McCloskey in attendance. She grew up playing in the grubby streets of the Gas House District, just north of New York's Lower East Side, in the heart of an Irish Catholic immigrant community. Mae was the oldest and, she would say, the smartest of three children. Her brother, Robert, was five years younger than she was, and her sister, Selma, nine.

The Gas House District was in the part of Manhattan dominated by giant gas storage tanks and rival gas companies. Located just north of the neighborhoods known today as Peter Cooper Village and Stuyvesant Town, the Gas House District was a relatively poor section, comprised of fluctuating immigrant populations: Jewish, German, Irish, Russian, and French.

Irish immigrants flowed into New York in the early nineteenth century, increasing more than six times over by the 1830s. Immigrant neighborhoods were crowded with the poor who moved upward and onward as soon as they were able. The competition for space, control, and leverage was intense. The rise of ethnic gangs began in this swirling melting pot, and crime rose along with them. Then the night grew brighter.

By the time Mae was born, electrical lighting was becoming increasingly popular in homes, and the gas companies that were located in the district no longer had a monopoly on providing gas for light, focusing instead on sales for cooking and heat.[2]

Methods and means of policing this morass were still being developed. Women's role? Initially none, but eventually something had to be done to care for the young women who were at risk victims and often criminals themselves. Mae was two years old when the city hired its first female employees. The New York City Police Department, recently dubbed "the finest," hired four women who were assigned as precinct matrons. Although they weren't considered to be "officially in the ranks," matrons were required to take the city's civil service exam, proving they were both mentally and physically capable of doing the job.[3]

Some of the matrons served in jails while others performed social work roles, expanding the accepted social practice of wife/mother/caregiver to broader custodial care, taking care of abandoned babies and lost children, and supporting runaway girls, young women forced into prostitution, or even petty thieves and pickpockets, plus the female prisoners.[4] Of course those who served in jails had the worst jobs, scrubbing out the cells after drunks and thieves had vacated them, leaving their litter and often a variety of bodily fluids behind. Plus, they were charged with keeping other areas of the police station clean. It was dirty work and often thankless. The officers weren't known for being the tidiest of men. Or the nicest.

It took another year before women were considered official members of the force.[5] It was a grudging acceptance, and true acceptance of women on the force took much longer. *Years* longer. *Decades* longer. Maybe even a century.

In the meantime, New York was a crowded, crime-ridden, and exciting hot mess. It was rife with competing factions, gangs, criminals, and politicians, all scuffling for a toehold on the ladder of success, celebrity, or even notoriety. It was a confusing mix of opportunity and danger that enticed runaways and opportunists, entrepreneurs, and masters of exploitation and trafficking— both in people and drugs.

Mae lived in a part of the city that was terrorized by street criminals, not just the Gas House Gang but also the Pug Uglies and the infamous Bowery Boys. Many gangs hailed from the slum area known as Five Points, south of Chinatown. While this area was south of the Gas House District, many gangs traversed large segments of the city.

The majority of these gangs originated in the nineteenth century, including the Bowery Boys, the Shirt Tails, and the Forty Thieves. Poor, violent, and dressed to kill, the Bowery Boys were known for their religious and political ambitions. They often clashed with Irish Catholic gangs and focused on campaigning for limits on immigration. The Gas House Gang was one well known in Mae's neighborhood. This gang's specialty was armed robbery, often committing between thirty and forty attacks a night. But there were literally hundreds of gangs in New York at the turn of the century: the Italian and Russian Mafias, the Irish mob, the Jewish American gangs, plus Black, Spanish-speaking, and Chinese gangs.[6]

Not surprisingly, Mae witnessed fights, assaults, thefts, and more on a daily basis. A few times, the wild boys from her parochial school tried to trip her up on her way to class, one block over. It was just boys being boys, especially when the nuns weren't looking.

One day, she saw them coming straight down the street toward her. It was her brother Robert's first year in school, and she would walk him over to the schoolyard before continuing on to the girl's school a couple of blocks over.

"Hey, Mae! You wanna buy a stick of gum?"

"Ha! Not from the likes of youse!" Mae knew that was how the boys got close to their marks. One distracted the victim by badgering him or her to buy gum while others picked pockets or ran off with purses. And just for fun, they enjoyed harassing any younger girls they could find. This neighbor boy, a couple of years older than eleven-year-old Mae, wasn't going to pull such an obvious ploy on her.

"Oh yeah?" His mouth turned down and Mae heard another boy run up behind her, his cheap shoes flapping, the sole coming loose. The others across the street began cheering him on.

Mae whispered to her brother, "Don't move, Bobby. Just step back." Wide-eyed, the little boy moved off the sidewalk. Mae knew he was shy and slow to make friends in his class. Bobby didn't need to feel bullied by the older boys. She shot him a glance, finger to her lips. "Shh."

Mae checked the boys' location out of the corner of her eye. When the shoe flapper was almost close enough to push the schoolbooks out from under her arm, she turned and clipped the little blond monster right on his ear. He fell hard on the sooty sidewalk, bouncing up on his rear.

"Ow!" He grabbed his head. "You can't do that." She could see tears in his eyes.

Bobby started to laugh, then clapped a hand over his mouth. Mae shushed him again. No need to shame the kid further. The little monster must have heard the laugh though. His face turned as red as a rotten tomato. He started to sputter, but Mae interrupted him, her foot on his big toe, sticking out from the rotten shoe.

"You ever come near me or my brother again, and I'll do you worse than that," Mae promised.

"Who do you think you are? You ain't no cop. You're just a girl." The boy struggled to get up, still clutching his bent ear. His friends were watching.

"I will be. One of these days, I will be a cop and I'll put you and your stupid little friends in jail. Now run on home to your mama." Mae turned and walked away. Bobby stepped up and grabbed Mae's hand. She was already his hero.

Those boys, from Saint Gabriel's boys school around the block, never bothered her again. But Mae kept watch. Much of daily life in the Gas House District took place in the streets, and from the front steps of her tenement building, Mae witnessed it all firsthand. Critics of nineteenth-century New York condemned the "monotonous brownstones," viewing them as a dull blight on the growing city's appeal.[7] But Mae loved her home, and the views were unbeatable.

Portrait of Mary Vermell, age seventeen.
(Photo courtesy of the Foley family.)

In 1895, aspiring politician Theodore Roosevelt assumed the role of commissioner on the newly installed board of police commissioners. He immediately began to reform the hiring process, emphasizing mental and physical abilities, not political influence. That same year, Minnie Gertrude Kelly became the first woman to serve as secretary to the police board. Change was slow to come, but as Mae and the city grew, women's roles changed too.

Roosevelt attacked the problems with the police department with his customary zeal, attempting reforms not only in personnel but in the city's customs. When he tried to close saloons on Sundays, the only day most working men could visit them, there was a considerable backlash. He only served as commissioner for two years; although his term was marked by constant upheaval and controversy, he was remembered as a force for good.[8]

His efforts helped pave the way for the modern police force, from the addition of telephone call boxes in neighborhoods to the development of station houses and a transport system to help officers arrive on the scene of an incident more quickly. While his efforts greatly improved the morale of officers, once he instituted a system for recognition for performance, it improved even more.[9]

By the time Mae was in high school, the city was leaning into the twentieth century and the bright new era of promise, modernization sprouting everywhere. Saint Gabriel's parochial school had been chartered as a two-year high school in 1894, the first high school of middle academic grade in the Archdiocese of New York. The boys' and girls' schools combined boasted 1,485 students with a mixed staff of Christian brothers, Sisters of Charity, and lay teachers.[10]

Even when Mae was still in high school, the parochial school's days were numbered. The neighborhood was continuing to move away from residential structures; the school closed in 1912. The church was demolished in preparation for the opening of the Queens-Midtown Tunnel in 1939. The tunnel access and exit span the area from Thirty-Seventh to Forty-Second Street, between First and Second Avenues. The city continued to expand and grow, swallowing some neighborhoods whole.[11]

New York was becoming a major city, those boroughs, villages, and neighborhoods consolidated into a single entity, New York City, mashing together the various competing cultures, old-country habits, languages, and idiosyncrasies. The consolidated NYPD was newly formed from a variety of local constabulary forces and began to adjust to its revised role with the same melting pot of personality conflicts, political frictions, and broad new opportunities.

As she walked to Saint Gabriel's Select School for Girls every day, Mae saw police on mounted patrol, then bicycles, and eventually horseless carriages. The police were having a hard time keeping up as the pace of crime increased. Mae tried not to laugh as she watched hapless officers on foot chasing criminals who escaped in shiny new automobiles.

Motorcycles didn't arrive in the force until 1911, when the police commissioner created the "Motorcycle Squad," part of the Street Traffic Regulation Bureau.[12] Then the cherry-red Indian motorcycles roared onto the streets and began to tame the mix of traffic violations, crimes against persons, and other varied forms of lawbreaking in New York's fast-moving traffic wilderness. The daily symphony from a thousand honking horns had begun.

For Mae, the city was getting not only louder but brighter and shining with promise. Traffic lights began to blink, bridges and tunnels were under construction, and a cosmopolitan new world was emerging. Skyscrapers were beginning to compete for space, crowding one another for prominence under the sea-blue sky. Mae's hometown was growing up.

When Mae graduated from Saint Gabriel's in 1904, she knew what she wanted to do. She was just seventeen but she had a plan. Now all she had to do was figure out how to make it work when no one else had.

CHAPTER 2
FOOT IN THE DOOR

Mae started working for the city right out of high school. She was lucky enough to have a recommendation that gave her a foot up on the ladder in landing that first job, but after that, she was determined to find her own way. Between the recommendation from the chief clerk in the New York Supreme Court and her grades and avowed work ethic, she was quickly hired as a clerk in the Tenement House Department, working in a settlement house. Mae's dad gave her a piece of advice at her graduation. "My girl, you may have had a bit of help in getting this job, but now you make it your own. And don't forget, you can never rely on anyone but yourself. You do right by *you*."

At age seventeen, Mae Foley was on her way.[1]

Settlement houses came about at the turn of the century, the result of New York's rapid transformation due to the tsunami of need created by nineteen million immigrants flooding into the city. The first settlement house was created in 1886, the city's response to the living conditions many faced. It wasn't just about the lack of housing and crime but also every other result of poverty and human need, including but not limited to hunger, lack of medical care and sanitation, the rise of sweat shops, and wages that were so low they couldn't even be termed sufficient to sustain a man or a woman, much less their family. There was no standard, no oversight, no regulation. The rich got richer, and the poor struggled to survive. When some immigrants finally found the wherewithal to move on, a new wave would move in, scrabbling to get a grip on life in America, far below the poverty line.

Settlement houses were envisioned as a resource for newcomers, providing advice, assistance, health and medical care, plus education. The settlement houses created New York's first kindergarten and one of the first playgrounds in the United States.[2] Settlement houses were part of a movement started primarily by nurses and other well-to-do women; they were frequently viewed suspiciously by the populace they were meant to help.

But having grown up in the Gas House District, Mae was accepted in her new role. She was one of their own. She learned a lot about the types of assistance that impoverished families not only needed but could get and how that kind of assistance could benefit children and impact their chances for a good future. It was an education in itself and a situation ideal for the likes of an ambitious young woman like Mae.

Her next jobs were also in Manhattan, as a case worker in the Welfare Department and as a probate clerk in the Surrogate's Court. New York's Surrogate's Courthouse building was brand new when Mae arrived on its doorstop. The Beaux-Arts style building was built over a period of eight years and opened its doors in 1907. Originally built to serve as a hall of records, the building served multiple purposes. Mae's office was on the fifth floor, along with a courtroom and offices. The court heard cases involving the affairs of decedents—probate, wills, and the administration of estates. It also dealt with adoptions and families involved in inheritance squabbles.[3]

Mae's education in the workings of New York social and familial needs continued. So far, her experiences had led her to understand how to help people after the fact—the facts being those of poverty, hunger, death in the family, or becoming victims of crime. She began to try and think about ways of preventing many of the social ills she had been witness to. Then she met a man.

John Henry Foley was fourteen years older than Mae when they met in 1904. She was eighteen to his thirty. He was a good-looking man, with reddish-blond hair and a hint of mischief in those clear blue eyes. He was a first generation American like her, but both his parents had come over from Ireland. Mae's mother was an Irish immigrant, and her father was French, but they lived in a predominantly Irish neighborhood in the Gas House District, and Mae knew all the sayings, songs, and history of the Irish migration to the new world.

John Foley was worldly too, a veteran of the Spanish-American War. Mae was very impressed at the photos of him in uniform. He looked so important. John served as a sergeant with the Twenty-Second Infantry Regiment of the New York Volunteers and spent his brief period of active service at Fort Schuyler in the Bronx. The unit didn't get any farther south than that during the short-lived conflict and mustered out on November 23, 1898.[4]

John had a good job as a machinist working on radiators, and he could dance. Mae liked his smile and his big heart. He was the kind of man who would save a kitten from falling out a window, who listened to her stories about the bad boys in her school and loved how she stuck up for her younger brother. They both wanted to build a New York that would be a more welcoming place for new citizens, and they talked about what they could do to help the city. It didn't take long for them to get beyond talking about their plans for New York's future to talking about their own—their likes, dislikes, and loves, in music, ice cream, movies, and ferry rides.

Then John invited Mae to visit one of his favorite spots, the Saratoga

Race Course in Saratoga Springs. They took the train one Saturday morning and carried a picnic lunch. It was a long trip, over two hundred miles but they talked the whole way and learned more about each other's views on life, love, and politics.

It was midafternoon by the time they arrived at the track. John enjoyed watching the horses run at the racetrack. He bet on a few too and lost. Then a jockey fell in one of the later races and was trampled underneath the horses' hooves. Mae felt her stomach twist as the unconscious man was picked up from where he lay facedown in the mud and carried off the track. John tried to make a joke about the dangers of racing. Mae didn't like it one bit.

"My God, John, this is barbaric. I don't want to watch any more. I want to go home."

John balked. He wasn't ready to leave yet. It would have changed their entire relationship to let it end on that note.

"Let's just have our lunch first, Mae."

"I'm not sure I can eat a thing," Mae said. "But I think I do need to sit down for a bit."

They walked to Congress Park, spread out their picnic blanket, and carefully unloaded the sandwiches Mae had packed for them.

Mae closed her eyes for a moment, enjoying the silence after the roar of the crowds at the track, the horses' fury at their competitors as they thundered by, then the collective outcry as the jockey fell.

Then she heard music.

"What's that, John?" Mae asked.

"Sounds like a carousel, I think." He dropped his sandwich and wiped his fingers on a napkin, pulling Mae to her feet. Together they sprinted toward the sound, then glimpsed the brightly painted horses in the sunlight, swirling away into one long circle of laughter, then coming around again for another.

"Oh, how lovely!" Mae exclaimed as they arrived at the ticket booth. She hadn't seen an authentic carousel before. "Let's ride!"

The carousel with its hand-carved and lush painted horses was brand new, built in 1904. Mae was enchanted, looking up to see the brass rails pumping up and down as the horses sailed around and the wooden racers moved ahead with an elegance she hadn't thought possible.

They rode the ride, again and again. By the time Mae and John finally got off the ride, they were both dizzy, not just from the nonstop pinging of carousel music and the spinning carousel disk itself but from the magic of that ride.

They held hands then and talked about the future—marriage, kids, careers. There would be other carousels to come—in Central Park, Luna Park on Coney Island, and in Queens, at Forest Park.[5] But first there was a major roadblock to consider in the road ahead.

That was John's first marriage. A divorced Catholic, John had four children with his ex-wife. Mae's dad wasn't happy with the notion of her dating a divorced man, not to mention a man who was fourteen years her senior, but Mae wasn't to be deterred. She had to take it slowly, convincing her parents that they were in love and planning to marry. They continued to plot and plan and look for carousels to ride together.

One evening, Mae and John sat side by side at one dance in the church hall and whispered to each other under the stern eyes of the nuns who patrolled the room with their rulers, looking for young men and women considering any impropriety.

"So, Johnny, tell me some more about your life in the army. Was it exciting?"

"Oh no, sweetheart. We didn't see any action at all. Just marched about and waited. That's what the army is all about, you know. Waiting and wondering what's next. Kind of like now. What's next for us?"

"No, really. What was it like? Didn't you feel like you were making a difference? Serving in wartime?"

John's look became serious. "We didn't do anything to help win the war. It was all over so quickly. I felt like I had tried to do something important but it just didn't work out. I'm not happy fixing appliances either. It's like…"

"You feel like you aren't making a difference." Mae finished his sentence.

"That's right. I want to do more. You understand?"

"I do. I want to make a difference too. For us. For our future. Our kids?"

"Our kids?" John laughed delightedly.

"That's what I said." Mae squeezed his hand.

They both chuckled, leaning in, until an older nun with a permanent frown slapped a ruler down between them and they moved apart, just as far as the nun's ruler indicated though—a mere twelve inches.

Mae and John were married on January 26, 1906, at the Church of Our Lady of the Scapular of Mount Carmel on East Twenty-Eighth Street. While still considered to be within the bounds of the Gas House District, this was John's church; he'd grown up about eight blocks south from Mae.

Mae was nineteen on her wedding day. Her matron of honor was a friend from work, Mrs. F. Hughes. John was thirty-two; his buddy George Anton served as his best man. While they were married at the church, they certainly weren't married in the church but in one of the offices behind the altar, and definitely without the church's approval. Mae was certain she could see the priest, Reverend C. J. Laffey, tsk-tsking at her throughout the brief service, muttering *divorce* under his breath.

She knew what she wanted though, and she wanted this man with the clear blue eyes and the same goals in life that she had. Mae stared right back at the priest until he looked down and away.

While John too was sure the scowl was meant for him, they both forgot all about the misgivings of the church and Mae's family and stepped out the back door of that church, starting out on their life together, facing forward. John found an apartment for them in Brooklyn, and Mae continued to work for the Surrogate's Court, albeit the one in Kings County—Brooklyn.

Mae got pregnant almost immediately. In October, their daughter Florence Agnes was born. Grace Claire followed four years later, in 1910. Two of John's older children lived with them, a grown son and daughter from his first marriage.

"I'm not really happy about this arrangement, you know," Mae told John one night. Husband and wife slept in one small bedroom, along with their two small girls. They had to whisper to have any kind of an adult conversation at all.

"Listen, Mae. Jimmy is going to pay rent, and Catherine can babysit the girls when they get a little older. How does that sound?"

Mae still didn't like it. At seventeen, John's son, James, had a job as a jockey, and John was starting to spend a lot of time with the lad at the track. But with six people crowded into one small apartment, even a few more pennies helped.

When she saw an announcement for children to audition for a small part in a Broadway play, Mae took both Florence and Grace over to Forty-Second Street for an audition. Like other visitors and out-of-town tourists, Mae was dazzled by the bright electric lights that advertised all the exotic offerings the Theater District had to offer. For twelve blocks, from Forty-Second to Fifty-Third Streets, electric signs and streetlights advertised their sophisticated entertainment options.[6] Baby Grace looked up wide-eyed at the lights, pointing out one sign after another. "It's the Great White Way, Gracie," Mae said. "Don't you want to be part of it all?"

Grace just nodded and laughed. Mae wanted to be part of it all too. Grace was the right age, at twenty-four months, and got the part. While Mae was thrilled at first with the check for Grace's acting, she was even more thrilled with her exposure to not only the bright lights but the inner workings of theater culture and the backstage family of actors and actresses she met. In short, Mae was starstruck.

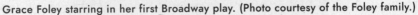

Grace Foley starring in her first Broadway play. (Photo courtesy of the Foley family.)

With the addition of Grace's acting wages, Mae was determined to find her family a real home. Eventually, they all moved to a house in Brooklyn. It even had a miniature yard out back for the girls to play in. One sunny morning in the spring of 1915, Mae shooed the two little blond girls out back and watched them out the kitchen window, sitting atop the picnic table with their dolls. Florence was seven, Grace three. There they sat, two innocent-looking Irish cherubs, with a smattering of cinnamon freckles across their little faces. Florence played quietly, murmuring to her doll. *A rule follower*, Mae thought.

Flo was quiet and reserved, but silly sometimes too. She could always make Mae laugh. But Grace… Her dolls were always dirty from being tossed about and living through wild adventures in the desert that was their sandbox. One day, she claimed her doll had foiled a bank robbery. She could always make Mae gasp.

"Where does she get this wild imagination?" John whispered in Mae's ear. He put his arms around her waist. Together they looked out the window. Now the little girls were on the swing, Flo pushing as Grace sailed back and forth, her doll clutched in one hand, even as she clung to the chains on either side of the swing.

"I have no idea," Mae said and smiled, but she knew exactly where Grace got her gumption and her no-holds-barred attitude. *Me*, she thought. And given her success on the stage, she also realized Grace was a born actress. Mae knew there would be trouble ahead with that one. She was a born storyteller with a growing iron will and a leaning toward outrageous fiction in her tall tales. "Probably gets it from you," Mae whispered. "She looks like a born gambler to me."

"Oh no, you don't! Sure and look at her lecturing those dolls. She gets all that fire from you. You don't fool me, Mama Mae. And while Gracie is a born leader, I think the quiet one is the one to watch. That Flo is either going to be a comedian or the governor of New York." He kissed her and Mae laughed.

Another hard kiss and a quick wink and he was out the door. With one ear open to listen for any sudden disagreements between the two girls, Mae sat reading the *Brooklyn Daily Eagle* at the breakfast table. Suddenly she stopped buttering her toast, the knife quivering in midair as she came across the incredible story of the one and sadly the only, Isabella Goodwin.

Isabella was the first female detective with the NYPD. No, wait. The paper called her "the best-known woman sleuth in the United States."[7] Mae swallowed hard, dropped her toast, and kept reading.

New York Police Commissioner Theodore Roosevelt hired Isabella as a matron in the 1890s, but the article explained that in 1912, she found a special assignment, serving as a scrubwoman in a boardinghouse, for six dollars a week. The new position was an upgrade from typical matron duties—cleaning out filthy jail cells, with their gallons of vomit, urine, and bloody messes.

Going undercover, Isabella was finally involved in actual police work. Her mission: find enough evidence to arrest Eddie "the Boob" Kinsman, a gangster who visited his girlfriend Annie at a run-down rooming house. Isabella didn't hesitate. She grabbed her scrub brush, put on her apron and kerchief, polished her Irish brogue, and got to work cooking, cleaning, and making new friends.[8]

Kinsman was supposedly one of the "taxi bandits," robbers who hijacked cabs and held up the occupants. One of his big heists was a $25,000 score, robbing a taxi packed with bank workers. The police didn't have cars then. They couldn't chase the thieves, just stood helpless on the sidewalks as thieves pulled away, waving goodbye. They needed someone on the inside. Someone like Isabella.

It wasn't just a one-day job. Isabella had to stay at the boardinghouse, eating scraps of food, sleeping in what she termed a "dark, wretched little hole,"[9] listening at keyholes and snooping at every opportunity. After a few long weeks, she got the information needed, and Kinsman was arrested. In return, the department awarded Isabella a first-grade detective shield. It was a case that had stumped over sixty detectives assigned to the case. Isabella Goodwin had made her point. Women couldn't just be policewomen. They could be *great* detectives.

Mae kept reading, her imagination racing. Incredibly, that case wasn't even Isabella's first rodeo. She was well regarded across the force long before the boardinghouse case and had gone undercover several times, exposing fake fortune tellers and other scam artists. She'd also posed as a degenerate gambler, setting up police raids of women's gambling parlors.

But she still wasn't a policewoman, Mae reasoned. She'd gone from being a matron to, well, becoming an actress. And she was rewarded for that. She may have been the first, Mae thought, but she wasn't a sworn officer before that promotion. Not a trained policewoman.

In a 1912 interview, Isabella acknowledged her role with the department was unusual and gave a nod to the culture of the time. "Despite my peculiar work, I try not to neglect my home. A woman's first duty is to her family and I have tried always to remember that."[10]

Even as a detective, Isabella was paid only about $1,000 a year, less than half what the male detectives made. But she loved the job. Isabella once said she was proud to "show just what a woman can do when the chance comes her way."[11]

Isabella wasn't the only role model Mae had read about recently. Officer Mary Boyd, serving in 1913, was recognized for breaking up a fight on a streetcar. She tossed the offender from the car and held him against a streetlight until backup arrived.

Mae wanted the chance to serve, and if Isabella Goodwin and Mary Boyd could do it, she could do it too. And they both had small children. Now she wanted it more than ever.

But her daughters were still young. Mae would have to wait.

CHAPTER 3
A SHOT OF PROGRESS

"Mae, can you take on this effort?" Police Inspector James Dwyer asked. "I know you can get this going. Maybe recruit some new members, teach them the ropes. It's the only way we're really going to make a difference in our neighborhoods. Keep the kiddies safe."

Mae was already well known to police leadership due to her background in social work and her advocacy for women and children. Dwyer had picked her for a good reason, having seen her in action at the police ball. He knew she could organize events, persuade her friends to join, and then teach them how to do the same. She could bring the numbers up fast. Mae would host soirees, sing a few Irish songs in her lilting voice, and the women in the audience would find themselves spellbound, ready to agree to anything she proposed.

"Yes, sir, I can do that," Mae stammered. She knew she sounded eager, but she just couldn't help it. "I'll get it done. You'll see."

Mae walked away in a daze. She'd made a promise with no idea how to get it done beyond her usual socials, so she organized a trial run, a pot-luck for friends. She knew about those from her church groups, friends, and neighbors. There would be food, a song, and then a little bit of a recruitment speech.

Mae worked her way through her neighborhood like she was campaigning for office. Energized and excited to prove herself, she went to work immediately. "Don't you want to come out, Mary Patricia?" she asked. "You can bring your sister too. Colleen has the twins now. She's interested in keeping the streets safe for those boys."

To another woman, she said, "Donna, didn't you say you would sing some Irish folk songs with me at my next event? It's going to be Saturday at the parish hall. You can bring your husband too. Oh, and be sure to invite all the ladies from your garden club."

Mae lassoed them all. She recognized this request for the career opportunity it was and quickly put together the plans for over two thousand women to serve in the Women's Police Reserve. She was the first president of the organization, holding the rank of captain. Mae was on her way, prying open the door to a job on the police force.

She charmed her female colleagues, brought them in, and then supervised their work. At first, it was all administrative, as mundane and boring as any office typing pool. But a precinct was more than a dusty, loud, explosive office. As the women prepared reports and summonses and typed up witness statements, they had to try to focus while all around them, milling patrolmen and detectives mixed with crying victims, suspects, and hardened criminals. There was chaos, clacking typewriters, cursing of the like that many had never heard in their quiet, sheltered lives before. Excitement too, plenty of excitement. The administrative work wasn't very challenging, but it was necessary, and it helped Mae in gaining the support of the male police leadership for what her girls could do. Soon there were new uniforms and pride in wearing them and marching along in the streets, chins up and eyes ready to seek out any and all affronts to the law.

The reserve program had begun in 1915 as an attempt to breathe new life into New York's citizenry's interest and participation in crime prevention. As a "neighborhood watch" kind of program, it wasn't very effective. Originally organized as a men's police reserve, it was already established, on paper at least, but according to Dwyer, it was languishing, lacking in leadership and direction. Adding women made the reserve more popular with the city's citizenry and increased the visibility of the police on the street.

Other organizations supporting women in law enforcement were also getting off the ground. With the blessing of the International Association of Chiefs of Police, the International Association of Policewomen flung open its doors in 1915 and began accepting members. The time was right, it seemed. Four years later, more than sixty police departments across the country had added female officers to their rolls. It was a start.[1]

Mae's beginning with the NYPD was right up her alley. She had freedom to organize the women's reserve as she saw fit and did things as she always had: her way.

"I was ready," she once said. "It was time for me to get moving. And I knew we could get the program moving and make a difference."

"We didn't talk much about it," Dwyer later recalled. "We just went ahead and did it. We got uniforms for them, drilled them, and then sent them out on public view."[2] The reserve was divided into two separate organizations. The Women's Police Training Corps was responsible for getting the volunteers ready to transfer over to the Women's Police Reserve as soon as they graduated. Every volunteer understood that their service was only temporary. Once the war ended, their services would no longer be needed. They knew it, they understood it going in, but they still hoped it wasn't going to happen that way.

Mae also spent time with the Women's Reserve Theatrical Unit, patrolling the streets near Broadway theaters, making sure that theatergoers were safe from street crime while out enjoying themselves. Many felt comfortable with Mae on the streets of Broadway, remembering her from the days when she brought in baby Grace to audition. Word spread. Mae Foley was going to look out for not only theater patrons but the actors, actresses, and backstage workers too. Mae took full advantage of the assignment and kept up with her growing cadre of friends in the theater.

She also became involved in patrolling the streets looking for runaway girls. It harkened back to her days with the settlement house, and thinking about teenagers sleeping on the streets made her think about her own daughters.

"These girls traveling to New York are so vulnerable! They think coming here to meet boys is all just a big thrill," Mae complained to John one evening when she returned home. The United States had entered World War I on April 6, 1917, and the city had been flooded with runaway teenaged girls ever since.

"Hmm." John was reading the newspaper. "Says here there's a Liberty Loan parade coming up on October 25. They have a real German U-boat in the parade. Now that ought to be a sight to see. You want to go, Mae? Take the girls?"

"John Henry Foley, are you listening to me? I'm talking about runaways."

John tried again. "Okay, if you don't want to go to the parade, the city is going to park the U-boat in Central Park. Right there in the Sheep Meadow. You can tour it if you buy war bonds. What do you think?" John looked up, made eye contact. It was a mistake.[3]

"Right there in the Sheep Meadow? John, there are young girls out there right now, far from home and getting into trouble." Mae stomped her foot for emphasis. As a parent, she knew how to talk to the excitable young girls who thought their trip to New York was all a big adventure. In the back of her mind in every encounter was the thought of her own two girls at home. "What would you do if Florence tried something like this?"

John got the message. He folded the newspaper and looked up.

"They're everywhere. Girls are coming here from all over the country and heading for those young sailors stationed here. We have to patrol Riverside Drive in Manhattan because women are getting assaulted near the naval training ship there."

"But—" John tried to get a word in.

"That's not all," Mae went on. If these youngsters aren't heading for Manhattan, they're on their way to the Brooklyn Navy Yard. They're finding these boys, and some are even getting tattoos of ships on their arms." Crude ones at that, she thought.

John opened his mouth.

"So what do we have to do?" Mae answered her own question. About the Women's Reserve, naturally. "We pluck them off the streets. Some are as young as thirteen, out on a lark. Others are runaways or just vagrants. Sometimes they haven't gotten into trouble yet. Other times, they are already working in a disreputable house. Trying to make enough money to survive. God help them if they get pregnant."

John's eyebrows rose.

"Let me tell you something, mister. We get them off the streets, clean them up, and ship them back to their parents. You've heard me talk about Mary Sullivan, right? She said, 'It's in part a case of protecting the girls from the boys and protecting the boys from the girls.'"[4] Mae crossed her arms. "Now what would you do if we found our Florence out on the streets with one of those sailors?"

John didn't say a word. He knew when it was best to let Mae continue.

"Well, first of all, I'd wallop her on her behind. Then I'd hug her and check her out all over. Make sure she hadn't been hurt. Then I'd warn the sailor to run for his life. After that, I'd haul her home in handcuffs and send her to the basement until she turned twenty-one."

John merely nodded.

Mae knew he believed her. Every word. Any sailor who came near her girls had better run. Unfortunately, one day there would be a sailor cruising into Grace's life.

By the time the United States entered World War I on April 6, 1917, the Women's Police Reserve was off and running. Mae's career, it seemed, was just beginning too. John was still working as a machinist but had taken a new job with the American Wringer Company, repairing washing machines. He had to register for the draft, but by that time, John was forty-five and his draft card noted that his build was stout. He wasn't likely to be called up.

Wartime New York meant far more opportunities for the female reserve officers to excel. Crime bumped up to a new level, and there were fewer male officers to respond. Inspector Dwyer agreed, saying, "The work of the police force, since the war began, has increased so much that it has become imperative to find relief and these women will be able to do a great deal" so that the male officers could respond to "larger and more urgent calls."[5]

For the most part, their work was still routine and mundane but necessary. In fact, Mae thought it was more like freeing the men from the chores they didn't want to do. For many of the women assigned to the reserve, their days were still packed with round after round of typing, filing, correspondence, court documents, and more. But it all had to be done.[6]

On the streets, it was a different story. Now mixed in with the criminals, Mae and her colleagues had to contend with the possibility of German spies, infiltrators, and a new generation of criminals, more determined and violent than ever before. It could be rough, and the criminals she approached were often unpredictable or drunk and vicious. "I could handle 'em all right," she later recalled. "I was a bit of a tough egg in those days."[7] The women of the reserve's daily routine included not only being on the lookout for criminal behavior but also watching for violations of food and fuel rationing.[8]

Yet the Women's Police Reserve was charged with another significant wartime duty—seeking out and exposing German spies operating in the city. These spies typically disguised themselves as women, and while they might have looked inconspicuous to most men, they didn't pass muster with the women. Mae lectured her colleagues on the signs of deception. "Look at the way she grips a purse or check to see if her hair color looks natural. She may not have paid attention to her corsage or jewelry. Maybe she even crosses her legs like a man would. You'll know when something doesn't look or smell right." A man, especially a spy, pretending to be a woman could never smell right.

Mae took them out on the subway one afternoon and pointed out the potential spies. Each of her colleagues paid attention to Mae's comments and made notes. Mae encouraged a few to actually question some of the suspicious-looking women. More than a few embarrassing situations resulted. "Well, I never!" One rather manly-looking woman with a prominent and very well-developed mustache stomped away from Mae's girls in a huff. Mae joked later that she probably went home to shave it off.

On a sweltering afternoon in late summer 1918, one of Mae's colleagues actually trapped a German spy on the subway. The restless traveler just didn't look right and, on a hot summer day, seemed to be sweating profusely in her white dress, her nose shiny and bright without even a lick of powder. The reserve volunteer didn't have arrest authority, so she waved over a policeman at the next stop; he arrested the so-called lady, who turned out to be an undercover spy working for the Germans.[9]

Meanwhile, Mae continued to rally support for the Women's Police

Reserve, and her reputation for getting things done continued to grow. In 1917, Captain Charles Northrup of the Seventy-Fourth Precinct in her home neighborhood of Brooklyn had asked for her help. Now it was personal, time to go all out for the home team. Mae promised him, "I'll do everything I can to make the Women's Police Reserve of the Seventy-Fourth Precinct the largest in Brooklyn."[10] Major Mary Farrall, president of the Women's Police Reserve in Brooklyn and Queens, knew Mae and lauded her work in organizing for more women to join.

They held meetings and patriotic rallies and gave presentations, snagging prominent judges, police captains, and district attorneys to address the potential volunteers. It was a matter of pride, and Mae was going to make sure her team was not only the biggest but the best. She was a great recruiter and spokesperson for the force. It was hard to say "No, thank you," when Mae Foley was asking for support.

It seemed like 1918 was a banner year for women in the NYPD. Six women were officially appointed as policewomen, and Mary Sullivan became the first woman to serve as a homicide detective. Later her adventures would become the subject of a radio program called *Police Woman*. A television series along the same lines would follow in the mid-1970s, but that was more fairy tale than fact.[11]

Mary Hamilton was appointed director of the newly formed Women's Police Bureau.[12] In 1921, she along with Rose Taylor, Ada Barry, Mary McGuire, and Minnie Earnest also founded the Policewomen's Endowment Association. And perhaps most importantly, Ellen O'Grady was appointed as the deputy commissioner of the Welfare Bureau of the NYPD, responsible for the protection and prevention of crimes against women and children.

In May 1918, the Women's Police Reserve joined the department in a parade through the streets of New York in front of several hundred thousand onlookers. Mae thought they looked smart in their snazzy uniforms—blue jackets and skirt, black shoes and cap, and a bow around the neck. But she felt the women were disrespected by the department leadership.

"This is outrageous," she muttered as the Women's Police Reserve, all 275 of them, waited anxiously on a side street for the main parade to pass by.

"Why couldn't we march in the entire parade?" A new volunteer asked.

"They probably thought we couldn't make it all the way. You know how weak women are, right?" Mae turned to look at her colleagues in the rows behind her. She shrilly added, "We might get tired if we have to march a few extra blocks and have to sit down and rest. Oh, poor me!"

They all had a laugh at that and turned the corner, heads held high as they joined the troop of marching officers as it crossed Broadway and Ninth Avenue. Local journalists proclaimed the women the "hit of the parade."[13]

Police parade on Broadway near Twelfth Street in New York City, May 12, 1918. (Library of Congress, Prints & Photographs Division, reproduction number 974.624, George Grantham Bain Collection.)

In January 1919, Mae was still working to support the Women's Police Reserve. She organized the first Police Reserve Ball, held at Coney Island. The Police Band and Police Glee Club both performed,[14] and the fundraiser was successful in raising money to purchase equipment for the reserve. Mae even performed a few Irish ditties at the event, hoping to be noticed by the senior officers. She had her eye on joining the regular force, but her kids were still young, and John didn't exactly approve of her ambitions. She still had work to do.

The numbers of regular policewomen continued to grow. On May 27, 1919, Police Commissioner Richard Enright appointed ten new policewomen to the force, now numbering twenty-eight women. They were directed to serve under Deputy Police Commissioner Ellen O'Grady. There was no civil service exam for them; the women were simply appointed and sworn in.

The new policewomen had arrest authority but no uniforms. The ten new officers were fanned out in neighborhoods across the city. Like male officers before them, they had their own beats. Their salary was $1,200 a year, a good wage at the time. A local newspaper noted carefully that the women "will not be uniformed…and will act as guardians of juvenile morals at dance halls, picnics, outings, moving picture shows and in all places where there is danger to the young of both sexes."[15]

The first African American policewomen were also in this group of ten, Cora Isabel Parchment and Lawton Bruce. May 1919 was a particularly good month for Cora. Two weeks earlier, she married Samuel Parchment, and they settled in Harlem. Her beat was the social welfare of the African American population in Harlem.[16] She remained with the NYPD for about four years before pursuing her true passion, teaching.

The other new appointees included Mrs. Lillian J. Leffler, Miss Hortense Thompson, Miss Helen Burns, and Mrs. Elizabeth Helms, all in Brooklyn.

Mrs. Lillian Gordon, Mrs. Sarah M. Ahearn, and Mrs. Rae Nicoletti were located in Manhattan. Mrs. Mary Cooney was from the Bronx.

Mae read the stories about those first appointments with envy. She carefully folded the newspaper to the page with the story about their appointment and left it on the breakfast table for John. He turned it over and set his coffee cup on top of it. Mae didn't say anything just then. She knew her time would come. Patience and persistence were going to pay off, she knew it. But once the Great War ended, the police reserves were quickly relegated to the background. Still greater changes were coming.

CHAPTER 4
PACKAGE DEAL

Mae had stuck with the reserves right up through 1922. The organization didn't fold at the end of World War I as planned, but it was slowly becoming obsolete. By then, she had turned thirty-six. John had just been pushed all the way over the hill to fifty, the half-century mark. The kids were fifteen and eleven. They could take care of themselves. It was now or never, she told herself.

"John, this is a great time for us both to make a career change." Mae watched John over the rim of her coffee cup and eased into the pitch. It was a big challenge she was proposing, but she was pretty sure he'd go for it. There wasn't a downside, after all.

"How so?" He turned back to the morning paper, looking at the results from yesterday's afternoon races. John had been known to place a bet or two on the horses. James, his son from his earlier marriage, was a jockey who raced at various tracks in New York. While John thought James's views on the horses and their owners gave him an inside edge on who might make it to the winner's circle, his picks usually didn't pan out.

John's favorite track was the Aqueduct in Queens, but he'd frequented a number of other venues: from Morris Park in the Bronx (it closed before they got married), to Gravesend and Sheepshead Bay in Brooklyn and Belmont. John had even taken a couple of trips upstate to Saratoga since their wedding, but the Aqueduct, now that was a nice track.[1]

"Listen to me. I've been talking to Inspector Dwyer and a couple of other police captains I know and—"

"Oh, not this police force nonsense again. You know I think your place is here. At home with the family. Now, the reserves is one thing but…" When she didn't react, he finally looked up and saw Mae's hand up in the air in a stop gesture. "What?" he asked flatly.

"That isn't what I was about to say at all. I've been talking with my connections on the force and asked them to recommend you for a position as a private detective."

"Detective?" John knew all about the famous Pinkerton National Detective Agency. It would be a dream job to work for them. "Like Pinkertons?"

"That's the one. I think you would make a great detective, John. And I've talked to them about where you could really make a difference too. Not just as a security guard, but as an undercover detective. After all, you know the jockeys and the horses. The racing lineup. You know the bookies. And you know all about how the gangsters frequent the races, the money laundering, the fraud. You've seen it. All of it. You've told me about it for years." She paused to let that sink in.

"That's true." He put the newspaper down. "Being a detective with Pinkerton! Well, well. I have to say, that would be a dream job."

"I know. And you would be so good at it too. Plus, it would mean a raise. There's only one thing."

"What's that?" John was suddenly suspicious.

"Pinkerton wants detectives with experience. So my bosses have arranged for you to work as a detective at Loeser's. Just for a couple of years."

"The department store? Fred Loeser's store in Manhattan?"

"No, the other store, the new one. Right here in Brooklyn. And it would mean a raise. They have ladies' dressing rooms, plus a brand-new escalator—I can't wait to see that—and even a whole floor set aside for management. You would have your own office. Plus, we would get a discount to shop there."

"Well, that's something." He nodded, chewing on the notion. "Now then. What's the catch?"

"I've known most of these men for at least five years now. They know what I've done for the Women's Reserve. And they know what I'm capable of—building a program, paying attention to details, getting things done, and not taking no for an answer. I never back down. You know what they said to me?"

"I have a pretty good idea where this is going." John sighed.

"That's right, John Foley. This is a package deal. You get a new career as a detective, and I get to join the police force. As a sworn officer. A policewoman. I checked and I think that together, with these promotions, we will be pulling in about three thousand dollars more a year."

"That's a lot of money," John said slowly. He appeared to consider her offer. Then he asked, "So they really came to you first? Not the other way around?"

"John, the NYPD takes care of its own. You remember that story about the detective, Isabella Goodwin?"

"How could I forget?" Mae talked about her all the time, like she was a star. Her husband was a roundsman with the force, a patrol leader. After he died and left her with four children, the department hired Isabella as a matron. Following her investigative success and sudden promotion, she was hailed as the first female detective in the world.[2] Mae told him that story at least once a week.

"That's right. The NYPD takes care of its own. They're taking care of me. And you."

"Well, I don't know. You might see some pretty unsavory characters, being on the police force."

"John, you can see unsavory things every day in the subway. And I've seen plenty of disreputable persons during my time in this city."

"I suppose that's true. But it's the violence I'm worried about."

"I can handle myself, John." Mae set her lips, folded her arms.

"Well, what if you had to face something like that riot last summer?"

"What riot?" Mae was puzzled. She couldn't remember reading about any riots in the city.

"The straw hat riot. It was last fall, remember? Downtown. Lasted full three days."

"You're going to have to remind me."

"It was groups of young men fighting over the hats. You know it isn't appropriate to wear straw hats in the fall, so young men—without hats, I might add—were stealing them right off the heads of those dandies who dared to wear them. Then fights broke out. This was all over Manhattan. I'm surprised you don't remember it."[3] John put a hand up to his lip, trying to tamp down a rogue smile.

"I must not have thought it was important," Mae said drily. "But since you're so concerned, I promise to never become involved in a hat riot. Or any riot for that matter. Especially if you are the one who starts it."

He laughed at that remark and said, "You've waited a long time for this, Mae. You're going to make a great policewoman."

Mae had won. The package deal was just too good for John to pass up. She applied for the NYPD the following day.

It was the full-throated roar of peacetime—the 1920s ushered in a new era in New York. The war was over; the boys were home. Then, on January 16, 1920, the New Year was a party no more. The Eighteenth Amendment to the Constitution was ratified by the states in 1919, and the Volstead Act, formally the National Prohibition Act, went into effect on January 17, 1920.[4]

The purpose of this ban on alcohol was to promote civility and curb bad behavior in public, plus stop petty criminals in their tracks, but the exact opposite happened. In Manhattan, Mayor Jimmy Walker went out with his wife and a string of chorus girls—at the same time. Speakeasies, the illicit private drinking clubs, popped up everywhere across the city, and gangs discovered new business opportunities.[5] The Roaring Twenties were everything a crime boss could ask for and more, an unprecedented time for impropriety in society.

They were also everything the NYPD wasn't prepared for and more. Crime plus the loosening of social mores from the wartime effort while the men were abroad meant women were beginning to come into their own. They could vote, smoke on the street, and make other choices for themselves, both good and bad.

Even before the official start date for Prohibition, the U.S. government enforced "wartime prohibition." Federal agents raided bars and hotels in New York, tamping down public drunkenness and the onslaught of petty crime it sponsored.[6] The rough-and-tumble clip joints of the time attracted more than their share of tourists, both fascinated and appalled by the sights of their fantasy New York nightlife being brought to life, just like many had only seen in the movies.

Far from improving morality and supporting American family life, passage of the Volstead Act only intensified all the opposite trends—from illicit bars to the underground sale of alcohol to the rise of rival gangs. It was a great time to be in law enforcement. There was definitely lots to do.

And to volunteer for. One of Mae's Women's Police Reserve colleagues, Captain Edna Pitkin, was a bit of an impulsive volunteer. One of Mae's early recruits to the force, Edna had been a Broadway star, and if asked, Mae would say she was a bit of a risk taker, not to mention a publicity hound. They ran into each other just as Mae was getting ready to submit her application.

"How have you been, Edna? Any new plays on tap?"

"Couple things in the works. You hear about the test I did for the department?"

Mae felt a sudden dread. "What test?" She hadn't heard about Edna taking any test. Was there a new test to take before joining the force? Why hadn't she heard of it?

"Well, they brought in this fellow, name of Leo Krause. He invented a bulletproof vest. Asked if anybody wanted to test it. So I volunteered."

"You didn't!" Mae's mouth hung open.

"I most certainly did. I put on the vest. By myself. It wasn't heavy at all. Only weighed twelve pounds. Then he shot me." Edna's voice rose. She looked around to see if others might be listening. Hoped they were.

"He what?" Mae couldn't believe what Edna was saying. She needed to hear it again.

"He shot me. Twice. With a .38 police revolver." Edna laughed at the look on Mae's face. "Didn't even tickle."

"Edna, you have to promise me something. When my husband comes with me to the holiday party, don't you tell him. Don't you mention this ever. Swear."

"Sure, Mae. I won't say a word." Edna looked a bit confused. She was proud of her efforts to help out the NYPD. They adopted the vest after all.[7]

By the time Mae was selected and started training, there were fifty-five women serving as full police officers on the force. The International Association of Chiefs of Police had just passed a resolution at their annual convention that women were essential to a modern police department. The movement to hire more women took on a new sense of urgency.[8]

While many New Yorkers and perhaps her own husband still thought *That's no job for a lady!*, Mae and the others just continued to prove them wrong. The NYPD Women's Bureau had their own precinct and their own training school. Women's roles in the department had been evolving for several years by the time Mary Hamilton was appointed to run the Women's Precinct. She'd been with the department since first volunteering to help with missing persons in 1917.

Ellen O'Grady claimed to be the first female detective. So did Mary Sullivan, but Ellen O'Grady had been a matron first, and Mary Sullivan hadn't been through basic police training. Additionally, as Mae knew, there were many who claimed to be the first policewoman or the first detective. One claimed to be the first to make an arrest, another the first to testify in court. To Mae, they were all firsts, all serving at about the same time. If she had to make a point, Mae would later say that she was the first detective from the first group of policewomen selected from the city's civil service list, and she was trained and educated as a policewoman before becoming a detective. Mae had never been a matron, a civilian working for the department. A sworn officer since 1923, she earned her detective shield. And she fulfilled her role every day on the job.

Mary Hamilton's view was different. She believed women were caregivers and women in policing should be focused on looking out for innocent young girls. That aligned policewomen with professionals in other socially acceptable professions, such as nursing and teaching.

The Women's Precinct was officially dedicated on May 3, 1921. When not working to build a training program for new policewomen, Mary Hamilton spent time redecorating her precinct building, terming it the "Hostess House." The curtains were frilly and the decor more like a parlor than a police station. It was just what Mary wanted. In just a few years, she would resign, her views out of step with the modern force, and the Women's Precinct would be forgotten.[9]

But while in charge of training, Hamilton was adamant that the trainees should have college equivalent education in physiology, psychology, law, and medicine. One journalist at the time described it as, "Here the women are instructed just as if in a college or a school with problems to work out on blackboards, tests to take, and homework to study."[10]

In December 1923, the department submitted their annual report to the city, detailing progress and accomplishments made during the year. The report stated, "In August twenty-three policewomen and ten patrolwomen were appointed on probation. They were assigned to the Training School for a thirty-day period of instruction. Particular stress was laid upon the laws relating to women and children."[11]

Mae excelled in the school, which provided both theory and practice in policing. She liked the practical side of her education much better, in particular the various methods for dealing with someone resisting arrest, how to handle a firearm, and the art and practice of jujitsu. There were fitness tests too, and more than one young woman had to go on a crash diet to pass. Mae breezed through every test and exceeded every expectation.

She was appointed on October 15, 1923, first on the list of eligible candidates. The day Mae was sworn in, she felt pride shining brighter than that gold shield pinned to her collar. John was there pointing out his wife to anyone who would listen, carrying his own badge and wearing a big smile.

Mae Foley's police shield was later made into a ring, worn by
her grandson John. (Photo courtesy of the Foley family.)

Mae's shield number was 73. In the 1920s, policewomen had their own
shields. Later all shields were the same; today the number is in the thirty
thousands.

The NYPD Annual Report for 1923 noted proudly, "During the year the
force of the Special Duty Division was increased…by the addition of sixty-
seven women." Yet it wasn't much of an accomplishment. The report compared New York's police numbers with its population of nearly 7 million to
the population of London with 7.5 million. There were 12,720 policemen
in New York compared with 21,647 in London. Adding sixty-seven women
meant that the department was about 8 percent female. The report stated,
"Policewomen are an absolute necessity in every modern and progressive
police organization, whether they are used to secure evidence, in certain kinds
of cases, or assigned to welfare work."[12]

There it stood.

CHAPTER 5

CAKE EATERS AND MASHERS

Mae was running late again, but she refused to rush. She simply needed to take her time, no mistakes today. Putting on lipstick in the tiny powder room off the kitchen was a challenge with the cracked mirror, but they were enjoying their new home, a real house, right there on Avenue I in Brooklyn. It was only six miles for John to drive to work at Loeser's department store where he relished his new position. He was officially the store detective, complete with an official permit enabling him to carry a service revolver. But the icing on her husband's cake was just for her; she truly enjoyed that employee discount. Mae didn't shop anywhere else while John was employed at Loeser's. Besides, she was finally a full-fledged policewoman. Thank goodness for her loving husband, John.

This was Grace Foley's favorite picture of her father. "My darling Daddy," she wrote on the back. (Photo courtesy of the Foley family.)

Ready for a new day on the job. That sure sounded good. *On the job.*

"Magic mirror on the wall, who is the comeliest of them all?" she asked herself aloud.

Thirteen-year-old Grace poked her head around the corner. "Mom, what does comeliest mean?" Grace stuck out an elbow. "Hey, stop it."

"Can I borrow your lipstick, Mom?" Sixteen-year-old Florence reached in over Grace's head, hand outstretched. *Gimme.*

"No, no lipstick. Not until you're out of high school." Mae pointed a finger at Florence and then Grace. "And you, missy, you know comeliest means pretty. I was picked for today because I look like a nice professional lady."

"Is that why you like cake eaters or just cake?" Florence hooted, backing away, then mimicked eating cake, puffing out her imaginary full cheeks.

"And, Mom, what's a masher? Do they mash up the cake?" Grace asked.

"They're the bad guys," Florence said. "Right, Mom?"

"Never you mind. Look, I have to run. Now get your things together, and don't be late for school. I don't want those nuns calling me again." She gave them both the stink eye, for all the good that would do. Hardened criminals folded and confessed when confronted with that hard look from her, but not her girls.

"John!" Mae called out. "Have a good day at work, hon!"

"Okay, you too. Girls, get a move on!"

Mae trotted along to the subway. Every day was different in this new assignment. That was what she liked the most. Never a dull or even slightly dull moment. She'd only been with the Masher Squad for a few days when New York mayor John Hylan visited police headquarters and noticed the squad drilling. They were all still new then, just getting to know one another, but the mayor was still impressed. "Who are these?" he asked a group of male detectives, waving his cane toward the gaggle of new policewomen.

Acting Police Commissioner John Leach explained. The Masher Squad had the mission of stopping perverts and other so-called mashers bent on harassing or assaulting women on the streets of New York, at subway stations, and even in movie theaters. Once the mayor heard the Masher Squad story, he said, "I can see I'll have to watch my step!"[1]

Luckily Mae and the other trainees didn't hear that comment or the mayor might have found himself being used as a surprise training aide. Mae noted the mayor whispering into the commissioner's ear from afar and the commissioner's uncomfortable look.

There had been an earlier incarnation of the Masher Squad, all male, but in 1924, Commissioner Enright resurrected the concept to include women. The news reports mentioned that the policewomen would be "easy on the eye of the male of the species" and that the new and improved Masher Squad would "not only have heart but mix in much common sense."[2]

The first women on the Masher Squad were Ellen Newman, Margaret Solon, Anne Murphy, and Catherine P. Brennan. Mae arrived next, along with another policewoman. Soon there were eight on the squad and then ten. It was too bad the mayor hadn't had the opportunity to watch the policewomen in their jujitsu training, Mae thought. She elbowed Catherine Brennan, who noticed the mayor still eyeing them.

"Bet you could shake the last nickel out of his pocket," Catherine said and elbowed Mae.

Mae laughed so hard she bent over, wheezing. Hylan was particularly ineffective as a mayor, with not much on his agenda other than keeping the cost of a subway fare from rising above five cents. In fact, he had only one speech prepared for his first mayoral campaign, about that fare. By the time of the election, nearly everyone was sick of hearing it.

Once Mae could finally speak again, she wiped her eyes and said to the trainees and the detectives, "Well, as long as he doesn't try to give any other speech, we are all fine."[3] Even the sober detectives chuckled at that one. Hylan had a reputation for not being either particularly intelligent or well spoken. Perhaps he sensed he was the subject of the joke the new police-women and the detectives were laughing at. He and the commissioner moved on quickly.

It was Mary Hamilton who instituted the requirement for women on the Masher Squad to learn the Japanese wrestling moves. She claimed that a well-trained policewoman, no matter how petite, "could throw a two-hundred-pound man over her shoulder like a sack of meal."[4] Mae enjoyed the training and, at the instructor's suggestion, began to develop her own signature move, one she could use at any time if threatened and execute it without thinking twice.

The media loved the Masher Squad. New York's newspapers were infatu-ated with the new organization, and many covered not only the squad's estab-lishment but their ongoing progress in making arrests. Mae and the four other policewomen assigned to the squad were selected by Mary Hamilton for their pretty looks, looking not a bit able to take on lecherous men on the street.[5] Five male detectives were also assigned to the squad. Coincidentally, all had the same first name, William, and thus became known as the "Willie boys."[6] The detectives were dressed as "cake eaters," 1920s slang for ladies' men— slick, well-dressed, and suave. Mae thought *slippery* was more like it.

Mae and her colleagues were deemed the best-looking new policewomen on the force, a.k.a. the comeliest of the department. They dressed nicely and took to the streets at both morning and evening rush hours. Of course, Mae was on the subway anyway, getting herself from Brooklyn to Manhattan. Her assigned turf was downtown, the Broadway beat, where she quickly made friends with actors, producers, and playwrights. They were well aware that if the theater-going public didn't find it safe to find their way to the bright lights of the rousing musicals and latest plays on offer, they could be forced to close. Mae was thus well appreciated and supported in the district.

Mae made friends, good lifelong friends, like the actress Dorothy Stickney and playwrights Howard Lindsay and Russel Crouse. These were friends she cared about, wanted to look out for, and not just resolve crime for but prevent and protect them from crime. She'd known many since her days with the reserve and kept an eye out for them. Mae spent her time on duty looking for men who stepped out of line, not just flirts but jostlers and not-so-sweet talkers. The newspapers called them curbside loafers, gay lotharios, lounge lizards, and worse.

Mae just called them stupid. She was at the Times Square Station at the beginning of rush hour one afternoon when she watched a young man jostle and annoy women waiting for their trains. He noticed her glare and sidled up to her with a smirk, whispering lewd little suggestions in her ear.

"How would you like to go out for a drink, sweetheart? Then we can go back to my place and maybe dance the tango?" He wiggled his eyebrows up and down.

Mae shrugged and turned away. Then he made the mistake of putting a hand on her shoulder.

Mae bristled and crooked a finger. One of the Willie boys hustled over and cuffed the masher, much to his surprise. Later, Mae told the magistrate in night court in great detail what he'd whispered into her ear. That included the details of each dance move in the so-called tango. The court reporter blushed and ducked her head. The defendant, a twenty-seven-year-old army veteran, objected, vehemently denying the charges until it was discovered he'd been convicted of the same type of misdemeanor a year earlier. He was sent to the workhouse for three months.

One of Mae's colleagues, Catherine Brennan, made a similar arrest at the

Lexington Station at about the same time. It only took her ten minutes to spot the man, assess his methods of sly approach, and peg him to be exactly what she thought he was: a masher. He would bump into women on the train, brush against their shoulders, appear to stagger and grab onto them to steady himself. If sitting, he would touch their knees with his and then grin, licking his lips expectantly. He was arrested too.[7]

But Mae's favorite story from her time with the Masher Squad concerned one arrest she made in Times Square on a night of dense fog and unrelenting rain. A masher was lurking in one of the phone booths at the subway station when Mae approached out of the yellowish circle of a streetlight. Much bolder than many of the mashers she typically dealt with, this one leaned out of the booth and called out to her just as she passed in front of him. "Hey lady, I've got something for you!" He then exposed himself, waving the invitation at her suggestively.

"I've got something for you too, mister!" Mae replied, slamming the door of the phone booth right onto what was undoubtedly the masher's biggest mistake of his lewd career. Mae got out her handcuffs and cuffed him on the spot. He wasn't able to put up much of a fight.

A flurry of news stories followed the arrests, reporters doing their job of shaming the perpetrators, warning the public, and deterring others with even remote thoughts of becoming a masher and trying to get away with it. In April 1924, Catherine Brennan made the first arrest in Brooklyn on the L train, collaring a man who denied pushing and then falling on women on the train.[8] Mae and Catherine weren't having a contest to see who could corral the most mashers but they were both taking a large swath of them off the streets and out of the subways.

When the New York subway system first opened in 1904, there were twenty-two stations. Many attracted riders with their elegant cast iron and glass entrances, but they also attracted the criminal element, as Mae saw on a near-daily basis. The Times Square area was her favorite location. While most New Yorkers despised the hustle and chaos of Times Square, Mae relished the air of excitement, the crowds, the tourists, and changing scenes. It was different every day.

Mae continued to make a difference all along her Broadway beat, where "she received her share of attention and made more than her share of arrests."[9] The others on the Masher Squad did too; there were plenty of mashers about, more than enough for each to find their own dozen or so to haul off to court. Director Mary Hamilton said primly, "People like to joke about the Masher Squad, but the need for such a squad is more urgent than the average citizen might suppose." She went on to explain, "The policewoman…is very much concerned with prevention work as well as with crime detection."[10]

As the arrests mounted, the success of the Masher Squad in curtailing petty annoyances in public began to spur other police departments across the country to create their own Masher Squads, from Washington, DC, to Chicago and Los Angeles. Still more followed suit.

Mae may have still been new to the force and in her first job, but she knew instinctively the importance of staying away from the headquarters and its politics. Besides, she'd joined to do her duty as a policewoman and had no aspirations to sit at a desk all day. She'd already done that once, thank you very much.

Mae had heard all about the two women at the top of the department. They had been fighting their own battles, but instead of collaring criminals, they had to contend with bureaucracy, corruption, and internal politics, not to mention the typical discrimination and misogyny.

First, there was Deputy Police Commissioner Ellen O'Grady. She had waged a bitter battle with Commissioner Enright ever since he assumed the position. It was a public battle, with sensationalized charges rippling back and forth between them in the newspapers. In January 1921, she said the department was "rife with politics and that everything was done to prevent any but the favored few from obtaining recognition."[11] She said that the commissioner treated her "like a dog" and undermined her "at every turn." She resigned in 1920. By the time Mae Foley joined the force, Mary Hamilton was acting in her stead.

Commissioner Enright finally departed for retirement by 1924 with Mary Hamilton quickly following him out the door, the separate Women's Precinct out along with her. During her time with the Women's Precinct, she had become convinced that women's place was not out patrolling the streets but at home in traditional caregiver roles.[12] She took her frilly curtains with her from the Women's Precinct house, but she had no doubt made improvements in the training and support for policewomen.

For his part, Enright had often been accused of corruption and failing to enforce Prohibition laws. His replacement, George McLaughlin, had a new view on how to deal with criminals: "Treat them rough." He emphasized putting real force into law enforcement, and it changed the tone and tenor of the entire department.

McLaughlin appointed Mary Sullivan as director of the Women's Police Bureau in 1926. Promoted to lieutenant upon her selection, she made her family proud. Police work was in her family's business. Her cousin worked for Scotland Yard, and two of her brothers were on the force; when she joined as a young widow in 1911, she knew the department would take care of her. The two Marys were as different as they could be though.

Mary Sullivan took on every assignment given and excelled at them all. She originally served as a matron, and because of her ability to assist the detectives in questioning female prisoners, she was soon given additional duties in detective work. Once, it was necessary for her to enter prison and remain as a prisoner for two weeks so she could observe a female prisoner associated with one of her cases.[13] By 1919, she was a full-fledged policewoman, but like Mary Hamilton, she too ran afoul of office politics. The new rank for women was considered comparable to that of patrolman. Mary had gone to the state house in Albany to advocate for the bill that created the status. The bosses weren't pleased by her activism, and she was demoted and moved to a new precinct. But she didn't quit and she didn't complain. She waited.

By the time she was called on to reorganize the Women's Bureau, Mary had been on the force for fifteen years and held just about every job a policewoman could have.[14] Her duties were described as providing leadership, oversight, and training for the policewomen in the department.

She would go on to have a thirty-year career with the force. When asked, she said, "I've found few things in the world more thrilling than the moment of revealing myself to a trapped and startled crook as a woman detective."[15]

But there were more changes to come for the NYPD and for policewomen. Many more. And Mae was at the heart of them.

CHAPTER 6
THE MAD HOUSE

One bright spring day in 1925, Mae ran into Chief Inspector Bill Leahy just outside the subway station at Times Square. She couldn't help glancing about in case there were any mashers lurking, especially in the telephone booths. Inspector Leahy took note of her casual surveillance.

"How's the Masher Squad these days, Mae?" Leahy grinned. "You getting those cake eaters off the street?" He paused to light a cigarette.

"Well, to tell you the truth, sir, they're a pretty predictable bunch. And they're like ants at a picnic. You squash a few and more keep on coming." Mae drilled him with her signature look. It was more like a demand than a hint, but he got the message.

"I hear you've made more than your share of arrests, Mae."

"I've done my part," she replied modestly.

"How would you like a new challenge? Do some detective work?"

"I'd like that a lot, Inspector. You know the saying, 'Along Broadway…it takes a skirt to catch a bootlegger.'"[1] Mae raised an eyebrow. Maybe there was indeed a job she could do with this special unit. And an opportunity to work as a detective? Yes, please.

"I hear you, Mae. You're a good cop, and we sure could sure use you on my squad. I'll talk to Mrs. Sullivan right away about getting you assigned."

"Thank you, sir." Mae was pleased but she knew John would be less than thrilled with her new assignment.

He'd moved on too, from the department store to Pinkerton. John was seeing a lot of booze being sold under the table during his rounds at the race-tracks. If there wasn't any effect on track security or any other obvious criminal activity taking place, John might just look the other way. But at the first hint of coercion, theft, bribery, or the like, he would have the hapless offenders hauled away. "Don't even try to ruin it for everyone else," he would tell them. Many of the bootleggers John dealt with were what he termed lowlifes. Mae know he wouldn't like her being involved with any of that.

Chief Inspector Leahy was as good as his word. He put in the request for Mae's transfer, but Mae was a bit surprised when Mary Sullivan asked her to report for an office call. Maybe it was an interview. She was going to be evaluated first.

Mae was ushered in quickly and found herself staring at Mary's decoration. She had been awarded the NYPD's Honor Legion a month earlier, on April 15, for her role in obtaining crucial information in a murder case. It was a particularly heinous crime; a sawdust salesman strangled his girlfriend with her own stockings. Gathering enough evidence to convict had forced Mary undercover again.

Founded in 1900, the Honor Legion is the oldest fraternal organization in the NYPD and is composed of officers who have been recognized for their deeds of valor while risking their own lives in the service. Mary Sullivan was the first female police officer to hold the award. Mae couldn't stop staring at it.[2]

"How do you feel about detective work, Mae?" Mary cleared her throat.

Mae blinked, noting that Mary had her personnel file in front of her on the desk.

"What? Oh, yes. I think I can make a difference in this job, Mrs. Sullivan." Mae sat up straighter, leaning in to the conversation. She thought understatement was the best road to take. No boasting. She'd heard through the grapevine that Mary had a penchant for taking down fortune tellers, as her own mother had fallen victim to several of them. Mae had made her own share of arrests of such scam artists too.

"Good, good. Well, of course you're going to make a difference. I've heard a lot of good things about your work. Just remember, as we say in the department, the title of 'detective' is a designation, not a rank. Technically any sergeant is your superior."[3]

"I'll remember that, ma'am," Mae replied. Mary was a lieutenant.

Despite her passion for the work, Mae didn't really know what to expect with the Special Service Squad. She envisioned her time as a Volstead Act enforcer as a high-class assignment. She'd seen the Broadway side of Prohibition during her time with the Masher Squad and heard stories of how undercover police detectives would infiltrate high-class establishments and smoothly take down the proprietors selling illicit booze. It *sounded* exciting.

Most of the speakeasies along Broadway were located not on Broadway but on the crosstown streets nearest to Times Square. The rumor at the station house was this was the area where some police officers took bribes and kickbacks from club owners in order to leave the business alone. The phrase "We're eating tenderloin tonight" was coined to celebrate a successful bribe, meaning the crooked officer was planning to order steak. Many were located along the side streets just off Broadway, while the less glamorous locations that served as distilleries and breweries set back a few blocks farther.

But Mae never got to see the top-shelf operation. She'd heard all about the big bust in November 1924 and hoped to take part in one similar. Then a number of policewomen and their male counterparts got dressed in evening gowns and tuxedoes and headed out to Mae's old masher beat, Broadway. In ones and twos, the police couples entered expensive restaurants and classy cafés near Times Square, ordering mixed drinks and wine. But when the alcohol arrived, they quickly flashed their badges, and happy hour was over. Many unhappy waiters, managers, and café owners were quickly escorted out to the waiting paddy wagons and hauled off to jail.[4]

Even that raid had been rescheduled several times. The talk around the station house after Mae arrived on board was that Mayor Walker would call the police commissioner when he planned to spend a night on the town and the commissioner would halt any planned raid rather than risk conflict with the mayor's office. He was corrupt but openly and brashly so. His nickname was "the Late Mayor" or "the Night Mayor." *Time* magazine reported that Walker "seldom appears before noon, if at all."[5] After all, Jimmy Walker was known for his love of barhopping, and he could show up unexpectedly at any bar near Times Square. Mae thought it put the NYPD solidly in the middle—right between the law at first base and the mayor trying to steal second. There was no winning that game.

But they did conduct one major raid and lived off the positive publicity from that night for as long as possible. Sadly, that was Mae's last exposure to the cosmopolitan New York nightclub scene. In fact, it was the only even slightly dressy evening Mae would have in her time with the Special Service Squad. The day-to-day policing of backdoor bootleggers was typically a dirty, squalid business. Mae saw more scams and robberies than she could count and had to use her nightstick too, prodding bootleggers until they poured their illicit booze out into the street.

The bullet-ridden cars, gang wars, and murders seemed to multiply faster than the police could put the perpetrators behind bars. The ants at the picnic comparison returned to Mae's mind time and again. But these ants were armed and vicious, and the picnic-goers kept increasing the demand. Plus, the smell of spilled booze mixed with drying blood seemed stuck in her nose. She witnessed plenty of leaking rot from basement stills, stabbings, beatings, and more.

It was estimated that there were anywhere from thirty thousand to one hundred thousand speakeasies in New York during Prohibition. One writer claimed, "These people and places filled a need which...seemed real enough at the time. While they lasted, the clubs contributed more than anything else to the mad house that was New York."[6]

Mae hoped to meet one of the more notorious speakeasy owners, Texas Guinan. An actress known for her roles in vaudeville and film, she was famous for her catchphrase, greeting clubgoers with the line, "Hello, suckers. Come on in and leave your wallet on the bar." Guinan flagrantly broke the law and was frequently arrested, but nothing ever stuck. She claimed she didn't own the Club Intime she ran so successfully, and the police couldn't prove otherwise. "I never take a drink and I never sell a drink. I'm paid to put on an act, and I put on an act."[7] Mae secretly admired her, a woman who lived her life large and loud, doing exactly what she wanted to do.

The Jazz Age had proven to be a balancing act—between morality and public drunkenness, between policing for the public good and charges for police brutality. For women, it meant that their new independence also came with a double dose of criticism, as though the changing times were something they had brought on just to benefit themselves. While there were fewer women involved in the production of illicit liquor than men, there were many women who frequented speakeasies, particularly the swanky ones. Hundreds of new ones sprang up along Broadway alone, catering to every class of customer. "Illegal booze, premarital sexual encounters, a body freed of Victorian restrictions in dress and manners and lifestyle were the definers of the 1920s as women began to come into their own," as one author put it.[8] They could vote too.

And as Mae knew, they could get arrested. When women were arrested, it meant policewomen were there at the station house to conduct the searches, do the fingerprinting, oversee the booking process. On more than a few occasions, Mae was also called on to search or even fingerprint a dead body.

By spring 1925, the war on the bootleggers hit a new high. Police Commissioner Richard Enright had earlier ordered a series of roundups of criminals at a number of well-known speakeasies, with arrests sometimes reaching more than one hundred suspects a night.[9]

Then it became routine. Raids on speakeasies had a rhythm and a pattern all their own, and once Mae got the hang of it, she felt the challenge fade a bit. She needed more. And the politics of Prohibition were being felt in the department.

She'd been with the squad for about a year when she asked for a transfer. It was time to gain some new experience. Busting the bootleggers had grown old in Mae's book, and it was well known on the force that the mayor didn't like Prohibition. The police commissioner didn't like Prohibition either and was known to have thought it kept the department from addressing more serious crimes. Even the governor, Theodore Roosevelt, was said not to like Prohibition, but he felt forced to address corruption in New York. Even thinking about the politics in her city gave Mae a headache bigger than one of Jimmy Walker's famous day-long hangovers, and yet the entire practice of Prohibition was deeply entrenched in them.

By the summer of 1925, Mae was attached to the Nineteenth Precinct in Manhattan. Located on Sixty-Seventh Street (later termed the Upper East

Side), the precinct straddled one of the most affluent and densely populated areas of the city. At that time the wealthy lived west of Lexington Avenue to Central Park and Fifth Avenue. The area east of Lexington, over to the East River, was densely populated with eastern European immigrants. The population mix didn't make the criminals any less wily or their crimes, whether petty larceny, robbery, or even murder, any less terrible.

She knew the Nineteenth from hunting bootleggers, but she could see there was a lot more going on than just illicit drinking on the Upper East Side. The Nineteenth Precinct's station house was a bustling station with a historic pedigree, having been in business since 1896. It was less than two miles from the Gas House District where Mae grew up.

She worked many long nights not just with escorting or frisking suspects but also in completing never-ending rounds of paperwork, making statements, testifying at arraignments, and checking on her charges. The new job was anything but routine. It had many of the same elements as her earlier job, but the danger level was ratcheted up just by the amount of crime, its diversity and complexity. This wasn't just booze and bar fights. The 1920s belonged to the brazen—the bandits, the fraudsters, the shysters, and the con men, both the lucky and the unlucky.[10]

One evening, Mae was called in to the holding cells to search a female prisoner. The patrol wagon had just brought her in, and she staggered along the narrow hallway, bouncing off the walls and stinking of whiskey.

"What's your name?" Mae asked her.

"Charlotte. Charlotte Flock." It didn't sound at all like *Flock*, the way she said it. The woman was swaying back and forth, boasting a wicked grin, her perfume a sour mix of cheap whiskey, beer, and cigarette smoke.

"What's your real name?" Mae began to thumb through the woman's purse, trying to avoid the ratty-looking hairbrush.

"Wouldn't you like to know?" The woman tried to look defiant, but she belched, stumbled, and nearly fell.

Mae took her arm. "Now, now. No reason to be like that. You're going to be here a while. At least until you sleep this off and your attitude improves."

"You can forget that, cop lady."

"Put your arms out," Mae ordered. "Now stand still."

Mae squatted and patted the woman down along her sides. When she looked up, there was a tiny revolver wavering a mere three inches from her nose. The barrel was a huge black tunnel, getting closer and closer.

"Get up," the woman said, waving the gun under Mae's eyes. "We're going to walk right on out of here. My man's waiting for me on the street."

"Well, he's going to be waiting for a long time." Mae grabbed the barrel of the revolver and twisted it hard. The woman grunted and tried to club Mae with the butt, but Mae wasn't having it. She had to use her favorite jujitsu move to get the woman to drop the gun, but once Mae had twisted her shoulder past its normal rotation and had it at the point of dislocation, the suspect didn't have a choice. The Kimura. Mae always liked that move.

Mae had her on her knees by then and kicked the gun away, finding a special holster secreted under the woman's clothes and twenty-seven additional rounds of ammunition in a pouch attached to her girdle. Mae took that too, plus the girdle and its strap for the holster.

Mae let out a deep breath, noticed her hands were shaking, just a wee bit. "I've never been closer to death," she recalled later.[11]

"What happened, Mae?" one of the male detectives asked her the next day as they were getting ready for roll call.

"Oh, there was a tussle," Mae said modestly. But it was the talk of the station. And Charlotte Flock, a.k.a. Katherine McDonald, a.k.a. Katherine McGuire and any number of other aliases, found herself with a massive hangover and three pending charges: carrying a concealed weapon, disorderly conduct, and intoxication.[12] Assaulting a police officer was then added on too.

The local papers had a rollicking good time reporting the story of Mae and the gun moll. One called Mae "the Amazon of New York" and modified photos of Mae and the suspect to make it look as though Mae was choking her.[13] Another article reported the suspect "fought like a wildcat!"[14]

AMAZON OF NEW YORK.—Fighting like a wildcat, Katherine Mc-Guire (right) had to be held in restraint by Policewoman Mae Foley, jiu jitsu expert, after being arrested on four charges, ranging from simple assault to violation of the Sullivan law. Search revealed concealed under her clothing a gun in a shoulder holster and twenty-seven cartridges which had been dumdummed.—*Story on page 3.*

"Amazon of New York" (*New York Daily News*, Sep. 25, 1925. P. 49.)

The jokes in the station house were as loud as a wildcat's wail and lasted for weeks. Some of the detectives even did a passable imitation of a Tarzan yell when they saw Mae coming through the precinct door in the morning. Tarzan movies were popular in the 1920s and it seemed fitting that Mae was the new star of New York's jungle, battling wildcats. "It's the Amazon woman," they would crow. Some would simply make catcalls. Specifically, loud and shrieking wildcat calls. Still others would purr in a menacing tone.

"Hey, Amazon!" a few would dare to greet her during the daily briefings. "Ooh! Don't twist my arm." They would pull up the corners of their jacket collars and pretend to hide their faces in fear while stepping slowly away, one arm hanging limp at their sides. "Help me please," they would whine weakly.

The teasing was all right at first, but after a while, Mae began to grit her teeth. Finally, she went to see the captain. Not to complain—Mae never complained. No, she had another request.

"Sir, I want to ask for a favor." She didn't even sit down in front of the captain's desk.

"What is it, Mae?" He looked up, trying to hide a smile. By now, everyone knew the story of Amazon woman.

"Come on, sir. You know what this is about." She looked down at him.

"Go ahead, Mae. Spit it out."

Whatever he had expected, it wasn't what Mae asked.

"All I want, Captain, is for the precinct to keep my name out of the papers. I don't need credit and I don't want recognition. Too much baggage comes with that. In the future, I just don't need to be mentioned at all."

There was a long moment of silence. "I understand, Mae. We don't need you to be famous." He wasn't smiling anymore.

"That's right, sir. I don't need that either. I could never do any undercover work if I was too well known."

"You're right, Mae. We will make sure the papers don't get in your business again."

"Thank you, sir." She was gone before he could even say "You're welcome."

Out in the hallway, Mae started toward the stairs when she heard a faint Tarzan yell emanating from the captain's office. Mae stiffened, cleared her throat, and kept on walking.

Mae didn't look back. She continued to do her job, take care of her family, and strive to make a difference every day. She guarded female prisoners, kept many from committing suicide or harming each other, and investigated dance halls, brothels, and sleazy hotels. When her Amazonian reputation cooled off, Mae went undercover more times than she could count, befriending women whose boyfriends, husbands, or bosses were bootleggers, gangsters, thieves, or murderers. And if the wives, girlfriends, and lovers didn't behave, well, she knew what to do about *that* too.

CHAPTER 7
WONDER YEARS

Mae stayed with the Nineteenth Precinct in Manhattan from 1925 through 1930. She loved the job, the people she worked with, and serving the city she grew up in. She was helping people, taking care of problems in neighborhoods where women felt unsafe, their children targets. She looked out for the female criminals in the jail too. No one was going to be abused on Mae's watch. The commute was a bit long, but she didn't mind. Home life was settled and comfortable. Things were going well, as things did…until they didn't.

Mae continued focus on the social welfare of New York's citizens, and as her daughters loped through adolescence, she found herself drawn to the crimes that tended to affect young women in particular. Her time on the Masher Squad had served a purpose in that regard. She was good at sniffing out men with ill intentions, had that knack for knowing when to observe and when it was necessary to insert herself in a situation and take charge.

More women were coming in the force then, and they were making their own way. Women were assigned to the Narcotics Squad, the Bureau of Missing Persons, and as detectives. That meant, regardless of the squad assignment, they found themselves doing quite a few bits of detective work. As Director Mary Sullivan noted, "In a way the women on the force have made their own jobs… It became obvious that women could keep a secret and were good impromptu actresses."[1] Of course Mae realized that from Ellen O'Grady onward, part of women's success in these undercover assignments was because no man, make that no male criminal, would have or could have suspected a woman of being capable of intelligence gathering, much less subterfuge. Often invisible and underestimated, they were perfect for undercover work, as Mae would well learn.

At the time, Mae, like so many others, had to feel her way with investigative techniques. By the mid-1920s, Mae realized she'd had little to no formal training since her introductory police course those many years earlier. Finally, in 1927, Mae and her contemporaries attended the "police college" for updates and cram courses in criminology, law, court procedures, social welfare, and first aid.[2] She actually chuckled out loud when one of the lieutenants claimed he was going to teach the women how to deal with potentially confrontational situations.

"What are you laughing at, Foley?" he asked.

"Sir, I have two teenage girls," she replied. "I deal with potentially confrontational situations every day when they get home from school."

The students all roared and Mae joined in. By that time, she'd also faced more than a few criminals armed with pistols, knives, shotguns, and a variety of other weapons, plus bad attitudes, foul mouths, and little to no sense of right or wrong, much less a conscience.

The New York Police Academy was located on the fourth floor of the police headquarters building at Broome and Centre Streets. The cops called it "the big white castle," a Beaux-Arts extravaganza, built in 1909 on the site where in the nineteenth century, the old Centre Market stood. The chief inspector's office was on the first floor, but Mae and her contemporaries were obliged to trudge up the stairs to their fourth-floor classrooms. Her training sessions there would be the last in that facility. In 1928, the offices of the police academy moved a block over to Broome Street.

Mae quickly grew familiar with the new location; she and her colleagues would visit the special shopping area behind the headquarters. There sat rows of gunsmiths and gun shops, all selling revolvers, pistols, and nightsticks to police officers visiting the HQ. In 1973, NYPD headquarters relocated to One Police Plaza. Rather than move the department's records to an archive, they "unceremoniously dumped a half-century worth of police records into the East River." That included records of not only accomplishments but also corruption. Fifty years of personnel records were dumped too, including the early records of Mae's career.[3]

Mae enjoyed the courses at the academy, although she undoubtedly could have taught many of them. The only part of the training she didn't like was the requirement to attend classes for a half day on Saturdays. That, Mae thought, was a bit too much. She valued her personal time with her family.

Despite the demands on her time, the classes in criminal law, code of criminal procedure, evidence, and testimony were all excellent. Many of the professors held advanced degrees, and they knew their material. There was still a focus on crime prevention, first aid, social work, and rehabilitation for policewomen, but Mae didn't mind that. Course field trips included visits to the juvenile and criminal courts. Even the advanced pistol course was welcome for the tips and reminders Mae knew she needed. She was very familiar with the basics of aiming, trigger control, care and cleaning of the revolver but found the science behind the classes in trajectory, velocity, and firearm evidence fascinating. As for the class on searching criminals and disarming suspects, Mae thought she had enough experience to teach that class herself.[4]

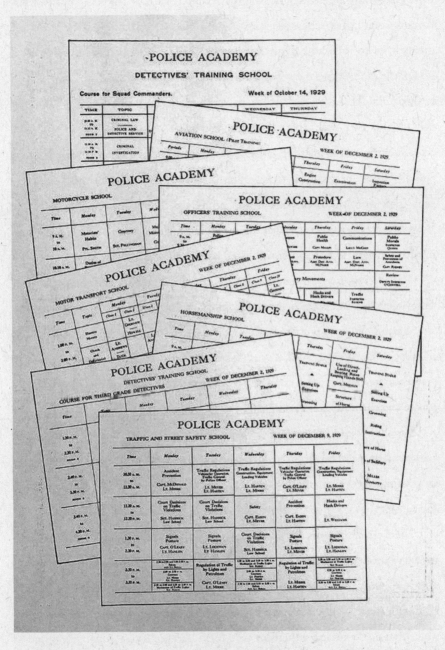

Sample training schedules as shown in the Police Academy (Institute of Police Science) Training Manual. *New York Police Academy: Enter to Learn... Go Forth to Serve* (New York: New York Police Department, 1933).

That training came along just in time. Criminals were becoming more inventive with their schemes, and Mae got to experience many of the latest and greatest in exotic scams firsthand. Fortune tellers now had accomplices who shook the tables where unwitting clients were seated for séances. They hid in a hallway and flicked light switches or stomped and moaned on the floor above the session. She was especially impressed with the woman who conducted séances with both hands seemingly placed quietly on the table. One hand was actually wooden; the charlatan's real hand was under the table, knocking away, seemingly from the "other side." Mae had a hard time restraining herself from laughing at this particular trick. She wondered if the woman had read about it in the papers. It was sometimes used by shoplifters.[5]

Preachers who claimed to speak to the devil as well as the Lord sometimes blew fire and promised relief from eternal damnation for only a few dollars. Faith healers sold colored water and claimed it could solve any problem, from syphilis to the common cold. Mae was torn. Sometimes she wanted to congratulate the scammers on their inventiveness, and she did. Right after the arrest and the cuffs were on tightly.

But her focus was always on the protect and defend side of her job. It seemed that so many scammers preyed on the weak and the poor. Mae was determined to put an emphasis on stopping those craven souls from doing any further harm.

Mae visited many fortune tellers across neighborhoods jammed with immigrants in tenements and squalid apartment buildings. She was always amazed at how many seemingly intelligent people relied on tarot cards, palm readers, or even a moaning dead relative from the spirit world to help them make decisions and learn their future would be a good one. Mae always had to stifle laughter when a seer would tell her in all seriousness, "You will travel one day," or "You are going to come into money." They would nod knowingly, and it was all Mae could do to not invoke the spirits herself and hope they would smack the lying *un*fortunate teller upside her head.

One day, a self-proclaimed psychic told her in a quavering falsetto, "You should be a detective." That was one of her most amusing cases, as she was able to reply sharply, "Oh, you have such insight. You really do have the third eye. Because I am a detective. And you, madam, are under arrest."

Mae always felt a sense of righteous accomplishment when she took down a fortune teller. She had heard Mary Sullivan tell her personal tale of why stopping these fraudsters was so important. When Mary was a child, her five-year-old brother wandered out of the house one day and never returned home. Mary and Mae talked several times about how her mother was so tortured by thoughts of potential abduction or worse that she would consult all kinds of so-called seers, hoping for some news, squandering the family's limited funds in the meantime. And sadly, nothing ever came of it.

There was even more fraud in the medical field. Unlicensed doctors and those claiming miraculous healing powers were in the same category, profiting off people's hope. Mae found many of these charlatans practicing in tenements similar to those where she had grown up. The poorest of people were often spending hundreds of dollars, their life fortunes, on supposed miracle cures for everything from stiff joints to enhancing fertility. Mae was issued charms, little prayers to put under her pillow, and vials of liquid to sprinkle in the four corners of her kitchen to break the spell of an evil curse. Some of the faith healers were no more than quacks, with their false degrees lining the walls of their so-called offices. Others with their supposed cures were truly dangerous practitioners. They did more than prey on people's fears with words; they actually attempted to do medical procedures. Sometimes the butchers worked not as midwives but abortionists. Those were the ones Mae targeted with gusto.

Shoplifters didn't interest her much. She'd heard more than her share of shoplifting tall tales from John. While some were amusing, like the woman who tried to hide a pack of napkins in her baby's carriage; others were more talented sleight of hand artists, and their thefts cost stores thousands. Mae heard stories about those women, "Beatrice the Shoplifting Queen" and "Light-Fingered Annie." Beatrice and Annie often worked as a team, one posing as lookout for the other. One of their favorite schemes involved heading into a department store wearing nothing underneath their heavy winter coats. Then one or the other would try on three or four dresses at once and walk out wearing them all.[6] Finally, sharp-eyed sales girls caught them in the act, and the queen went to prison.

Mae wanted to stop them all, every one of the inventive criminals she came up against, no matter how ingenuous. They were of every type and size, all scheming to make money with every possible scam imaginable. Yet much like before, Mae was ready for something new. Not just because it hurt her deeply to see young women who became addicted to drugs and were forced to resort to those petty crimes like fortune-telling, faith healing, or shoplifting to pay for their habits. She also wanted to break into bigger, harder crimes. She found it was the hardened criminals who interested her the most.

Mae preached stories of these crimes and their punishments to her daughters so often they became numb to the lessons she was trying to relay. That chafed on Mae's good humor, but not as much as the realization that she too was becoming both numb and affected by all the crime she witnessed on a daily basis.

She was beginning to think ill of nearly everyone she met, even if it was one of the kids' new teachers at school or a nice clerk in the grocery store. She'd eye them up and down, wondering what they were really up to, whether they had a weapon, or whether they were going to try to scam her. She began to worry in every encounter. What if that nice man behind the deli counter was actually a shyster of some kind or a thief? Mae clutched her purse to her side. Or a murderer? He certainly knew how to use a knife.

She needed a break from her own suspicious mind.

"John, I've been thinking. Now that you're with Pinkerton, we both make decent salaries and we've never even had a real honeymoon." It wasn't exactly the surest way to ease him into a discussion, but Mae thought maybe a little shock treatment might work. Just a tip on dealing with suspects she'd picked up in school.

"What? You want to go on a honeymoon? Now?" John looked at her, wild-eyed.

"No, honey, I want to go on a *trip*. I want to travel. See the world. I'm turning forty this year, and I've never been outside New York."

"Aw, Mae, come on, honey. We can go to Niagara Falls if you want. Or up to Saratoga."

"I'm not talking about hanging out at a racetrack. I've seen Saratoga and Niagara Falls. I don't need to go there again. I want to see something new." Mae drummed her fingers on the Formica tabletop.

John sighed and took the bait with resignation. "Like what?"

"Like maybe someplace in Europe. Go to London and see Buckingham Palace and the changing of the guard. Or Paris and the Eiffel Tower. I'd like that. Or even something really exotic, like Egypt. We could climb the pyramids."

"Okay. Okay, I get the idea. But, Mae, you know I'm not much for sightseeing. If you really want to go, why don't you just go by yourself? Or take a girlfriend along. You have what, at least two weeks of vacation coming to you, right?"

"Three. I saved some vacation days from last year." Not like she ever used them for anything.

"Well then, you just plan to go on ahead. I'll stay home with the girls."

"Okay, John. I think I'll do just that. I've got my passport application all ready to go." That settled it then. Mae didn't think he'd want to get a passport. After all, he'd have to put down his real age on paper, something John didn't like admitting. He even fudged his age on his weapons' permits.

So Mae took off, sometimes with a fellow policewoman who also wanted to get away, other times with pals from Broadway. If no one wanted to accompany her on an adventure, she simply went alone. And she fell in love with the romance of travel itself, meeting new people in exotic places, sailing to European ports, the excitement of cruise ships with their formal dinners, afternoon teas, and officers in splendid white uniforms. She would sit in a lounge chair on deck, wrapped in a blanket, hidden under a large hat and sunglasses, and watch the parade of passengers pass by. It was excellent entertainment, the men in their three-piece suits, all with slim, snooty women on their arms, swinging their mink stoles and fingering their new pearls. The stories she made up about each of the couples, groups, or their children probably exceeded the boundaries of what was possible, much less appropriate. But the ideas that some of them could be international spies, subjects of intrigue, or characters straight out of an Agatha Christie novel kept Mae intrigued.

Of course, she took time for a nap as well. How glorious to drift off into a dream while the ship rocked gently and Mae knew her watch was put away in the cabin safe. She didn't have to be anywhere at a certain time. No one was depending on her, calling her, demanding her presence. It was an endlessly streaming sweetheart of a weekend, with no obligations, no requirements, no guilt. She could replay in her mind the days when she and John were a new young couple. She could enjoy it all again.

On rainy days, she napped in her first-class cabin, listening to the wind tossing sheets of water at her door, demanding she come out on deck so she could be drenched. Her cabin was spacious with its luxurious linens, beautiful wallpaper, and basket of French soaps that smelled of lavender. The orchestra played every night; there were ballroom dancing and daily activities like deck tennis and napkin folding, although the spoon and egg races were simply silly, she thought. It was a fantasy life, living on a ship, and Mae felt like royalty when she traveled.

Each evening, Mae liked dressing for dinner, descending the grand staircase and waltzing into the formal dining room. She enjoyed trying new foods, learning bits of new languages. The elegant cruising life was like being a secret celebrity, and she fell in love with it. From then on, in just about every year following 1927, she went somewhere new, living out her dream of luxury, if only for a few weeks once a year.

But not the next year, because 1928 was shattering for Mae. Just four days into January's chilly welcome, John Henry Foley dropped dead of a heart attack, right there in their living room, cigar in hand. But it was still a shock, a terrible shock. And despite the cigar habit, the few extra pounds he carried, and maybe an Irish fondness for whiskey, Mae had never seen it coming. Apparently, John hadn't either, or he would have changed his ways, Mae thought.

According to custom in both Mae's and John's Irish families, the funeral was held at their home on Avenue I in Brooklyn. It was followed by a requiem mass at their neighborhood church, St. Rose of Lima, then burial in Calvary Cemetery in Queens. Even in 1928, the Catholic burial ground was huge, sprawling over three hundred acres and growing fast enough to claim the title of the largest cemetery in the United States by the end of the twentieth century.[7] A city of the dead, Calvary claimed to host over three million graves by then.

The graveside service was the hardest on Mae. The girls held her up while she wiped her eyes and the priest showered John's casket with holy water. The girls were silent, shocked. It wasn't like they were too young to understand. Florence had just turned twenty-one, and Grace was seventeen. They were adults and would be leaving the nest soon anyway.

But Mae felt too young to be a widow. Too young for all the decisions, the paperwork, the house. Even ordering a veteran's headstone for John was an ordeal. Everything weighed on her; each task felt like him dying all over again, and with each requirement—the taxes, the insurance, the headstone— she felt like she wanted to just die too. The trivial and the important, the baggage of death dragged her down not just through the rest of that day but all through the long and lonely year and on into 1929. She still worked, did her job, patrolled, investigated, arrested, and testified. But regrets held tight to her with those chains, clanking behind her with all the memories that she couldn't just reroute, change, or even hide from herself, packed away in the unused closet at the back of her mind. Her parents were gone, her younger brother and sister too far away to be of much help, much less able to provide a shoulder. Mae had never felt so alone.

On October 24, 1929, a day later known as Black Thursday, the stock market crashed. In just one day, the United States lost in financial solvency the equivalent to what it had spent on the entirety of World War I.[8]

One of the sergeants in Mae's precinct dashed into the lieutenant's office to report he'd seen a man on a building, getting ready to jump while a crowd watched. Mae heard his shrill voice, relating what he'd seen, and walked in.

"I'm afraid this is just the beginning," she said.

"And I'm afraid you're right," he replied.

"What do you think that means for us?" Mae asked. She was thinking of her girls. Their future. Her future.

"City needs its police. Now more than ever." The detective shrugged.

"We have job security, that's for sure," Mae replied. The NYPD would daily prove their commitment to the public's welfare by providing food, clothing, fuel, and even job opportunities to the needy. They also set up a relief fund.[9]

But Mae wasn't prepared for what was yet to come, the waves of hunger, joblessness, and despair as the Depression took hold of America and held her by the throat. It was to be expected, she thought later. The explosion of street protests and crime was the result of a level of desperation and a fear unknown before the Depression hit. And the volume of theft, robbery, and the attendant violence seemed to ratchet up each day. On her way to work each morning, she could spot at least twenty small stands on the street, destitute people selling apples in order to make a few pennies. According to some estimates, at least six thousand people a day were selling apples on the streets of New York.[10]

In Manhattan, the district attorney's office set up an undercover unit to fight organized crime and gangs that were using this time of devastation to try and capitalize on the misfortunes of others. District Attorney Thomas E. Dewey knew which policewoman he wanted to join his team.

CHAPTER 8
LIVE BAIT

As the Depression continued to mark the 1930s as their own, Mae decided she needed a fresh start, shaking up everything in her personal life. She was determined that the hard times wouldn't own her. First, she sold the house in Brooklyn for a tidy profit and moved herself and her two daughters to an apartment on Forty-Seventh Street in Astoria. It was a good neighborhood, a nice apartment, but it just didn't seem like the right fit. The new place felt like a thrift-shop sweater, scratchy and tight in some places, loose and full of holes in others. She just didn't belong there.

So in 1930, they moved again, this time to Woodside, just about three miles south of Astoria. It wasn't that far away but different enough, and maybe a few blocks further east. Mae felt herself gradually letting go of Brooklyn and venturing further afield. Moving had become a habit by then for Mae and the girls, just as it had been for many New York families for nearly one hundred years. Since the mid-nineteenth century, leases were typically negotiated between tenant and landlord annually. When no agreement could be reached, renters were forced to vacate their lodgings and move. The season for negotiations and moving culminated by the end of April. By the mid-nineteenth century, moving day was usually May 1, "the day on which every person is compelled by law to move."[1]

It was a custom begun with the notion of raising or even the occasional lowering of rents. On February 1, notices would pass between landlord and tenant, and by the end of the quarter, if no agreement could be reached, the office, apartment, or shop would change hands, a slamming door marking the certain end of the lease year.[2] Mae had moved a number of times in her childhood, her father negotiating rents with a bevy of landlords, ranging from the generous to the unscrupulous. She actually liked the process of the move: cleaning up, clearing out, something new coming. Moving day itself was kind of exciting—chaos in the streets with moving trucks and wagons clogging traffic, lots of hand gestures and police trying to direct cars around the loading and unloading vans. Families with nothing more than handcarts and wheelbarrows to haul their worldly goods from one walk-up to another wove in and out among the carnage, dropping suitcases, lamps, and dishes along the way. There was always yelling, crying children, cursing, some fighting, and even a handful of good-natured neighbors helping each other. But it was tiring, even if the family only moved a few blocks from one residence to another. Sometimes Mae wanted to change schools, but her mother wouldn't hear of it. Catholic school it was.

By the beginning of the twentieth century, moving day had migrated from May to October. Mae's successive moves following John's death in 1928 still followed the familiar pattern. The city's moving day activity slowed with the arrival of the Depression, as many families didn't have the funds to pay movers. One way the city began to track moves was through the transfer of utilities, primarily the telephone. In October 1930, the New York Telephone Company received 30,430 requests for changes in telephones. Just one year earlier, prior to the Depression, there were 128,000 moving day changes.[3]

Mae had her new telephone hooked up and the boxes unpacked, but she didn't feel settled in Woodside either. By 1933, she began to hear about a brand-new neighborhood that sounded fresh and appealing.

Advertisements for the up-and-coming Jackson Heights neighborhood in Queens were beginning to flood the radio waves. The ads were like a cool breeze on the top deck of a cruise ship, appealing to Mae's sense of adventure and travel cravings yet keeping the notion of a cozy home to return to. One ad that enticed her said, "Seek recreation and the daily comfort of the home removed from the congested part of the city, right at the boundaries of God's great outdoors, and within a few minutes by subway from the business section of Manhattan... Get away from the solid masses of brick."[4]

Get away... Many of Mae's Broadway cronies were moving to that area in Queens too; it was a quick trip to Times Square on the number 7 Train, and the pictures of the lineup of connected ground-floor apartments in Jackson Heights reminded her of the rows of English cottages she'd seen in Stratford-on-Avon, cozy and cute with their climbing rose bushes and sweet little patches of green. Just looking at the pictures of those tidy homes brought back memories from her trip to Shakespeare's birthplace in England.

Having grown up in Manhattan, then having lived in five different places in Brooklyn, all those residences were marked by massive walls of brick, then more brick in Queens. The new location in Jackson Heights felt like a breath of fresh air, not merely a few miles away from their old neighborhood. The girls—well, they weren't girls anymore—had more room in the garden apartment home, and Mae could call the new place all her own. Their little attached cottage was on Eighty-Second Street in Jackson Heights, Queens, an ethnically diverse neighborhood with good shopping and quick access to the Jackson Heights subway station. At nearly eighteen hundred square feet, it was finally a perfect fit.

She changed jobs too, transferring to the 108th Precinct in Queens. Her new assignment: detective on the Homicide Squad. Every precinct had its own team of detectives who shared the station house with the uniformed officers but generally kept to their own space. Typically, they took on all types of cases. When there were no homicides to work, the menu was definitely packed with other options.[5] The Queens precinct may not have seemed as prestigious as her former post in Manhattan, but it felt like a good fit to Mae. She was just getting settled in her new home when a deadly case came up that she would remember for the rest of her career.

The first murder occurred on the night of June 11, 1930. A thirty-nine-year-old grocer named Joe Mozynski drove to the College Point area of Queens with his girlfriend. They parked in a dark lane, heavily shaded with trees. Joe's wife didn't know he was out for a good time. As the couple were engaged in foreplay, a man approached the driver's side window and, without a word, shot Joe dead. The killer then turned to the woman in the passenger seat. Catherine May was in shock and unable to even speak a word. The killer pulled her into the back seat and raped her. Then he courteously opened the passenger door and, with a bow and a flourish, escorted the stunned and unlucky girlfriend, Catherine May, to a nearby bus stop.

The killer wrote to the newspapers following the first murder, saying he was part of a group called "the Red Diamond of Russia" and had committed the murder while on a "secret mission." The killer said there would be at least fourteen more murders until he was satisfied. The letter was signed 3X.

Then on June 16, twenty-six year-old Noel Sowley was shot while sitting in a parked car with his girlfriend, Betty Ring. He too was married and stepping out on his wife. The unfortunate girlfriend also witnessed the shooting at close range, and once she stopped screaming, the killer helped her from the car and escorted her to a local bus stop. The killer sent another letter to the police, stating that he was done killing.[6]

Who could believe that? After the second murder, in the 108th Precinct's district, the chief of detectives, Inspector John Gallagher, came up with a plan. A few detectives, meaning Mae, Detective Thomas J. Layden, and the inspector himself, would conduct a stakeout, see if they could lure the killer out in the open. Mae knew exactly what that meant. She was going to be the bait. Well, half of the bait anyway. But definitely still wriggling on the hook.

The killer had promised he would keep on killing until he got what he wanted, the return of some mysterious documents. Then he said he was done. The public was both confused and frightened. The police were baffled—there wasn't a clue about who the murderer was or why he'd started this killing spree. Maybe it was an escapee from a nearby mental hospital, some of the detectives said. But that was just a guess.

With everyone on edge for the past week, the second killing pushed the anxiety level into overdrive. Just that morning, the precinct received a letter from the killer. "No cause for worry," the letter concluded; 3X was "mission complete." The local newspapers were in a frenzy of guessing and stirring up more fears.[7]

Back at the station house, Tom Layden had blurted out, "Well, good. We don't have to go out tonight then. No use in being sitting ducks if we don't have to. Right, Mae?" Of course it was always going to be Mae. She was the only female detective on the Homicide Squad. Hell, she was the only female officer in the precinct.

"Of course we have to go out there," Mae snorted. "Just because he sent us a letter doesn't mean we have to believe him. You believe everything a crazy killer says?"

A couple of the other detectives chuckled.

"Boss?" Tom turned to their inspector.

"Whatsa matter, Tom? You afraid to go out in the dark? Or don't you want to sit in a parked car with Mae? She'll watch out for you."

"That's right," Mae chimed in. "You boys just take a nap. I'll watch out for you."

Their fellow officers roared. But it was true. They went out that night, June 17.

From a distance, it probably looked like they were kissing. Mae hoped so. She and the other detective were parked on a dark, lonely road near Hillcrest Golf Course. It had a reputation as a local lover's lane, but that didn't last long. The remote site later became part of the St. John's University campus.

Mae found herself looking around nervously. She squirmed in her seat. She really wanted to look out the window of the darkened sedan that one her partner had requisitioned from the motor pool. It smelled of stale cigarettes and Chinese takeout. Mae rolled down the window and took a deep breath. She scanned the wood line. Her companion, the driver, sat slumped against her. Mae thought she heard a slight snore. Tom must have had a hard day at work. She huffed and elbowed him, but he just grunted and swatted at her hand.

Mae chanced a quick glance in the rearview mirror. Nothing. Inspector Gallagher was out there somewhere in the bushes, watching for the approach of a deadly killer. Mae hoped he wasn't snoozing on the job like Tom.

So there they sat, Mae hoping yet not hoping that the 3X murderer would pay a visit. Her arm was going to sleep. She shifted in her seat when a shadow appeared out of the darkness, sidling up to the driver's side door. A man jerked the door open and shouted, "This is a holdup!"

Mae saw the facts of the matter in close-up living color. There was a very large and very ugly pistol pointed right at her face. Her eyes crossed as it waved back and forth.

"What?" Tom croaked. He woke up groggy and unfocused, seemingly unable to understand what was going on. Mae's hand was around her own .38

revolver when the inspector materialized out of the darkness and shoved his service weapon into the would-be robber's back.

"Put the gun down! Now!" He ordered, one hand on the man's collar.

Jerked backward and away from the car window, the robber had no choice but to drop his pistol. Mae was out of that car so fast, Tom rolled over on his side, arms flailing like a crab. Mae and the inspector got the man on the ground, cuffed him, and were stepping him away toward her colleague's police car when Tom trotted up behind them. He stopped to rub the sleep from his eyes.

"Hey, you two," he said. "Why didn't you tell me what was happening, Mae?"

"Day late, dollar short," Mae replied. Nothing else to say. Her grip on the robber's neck tightened.

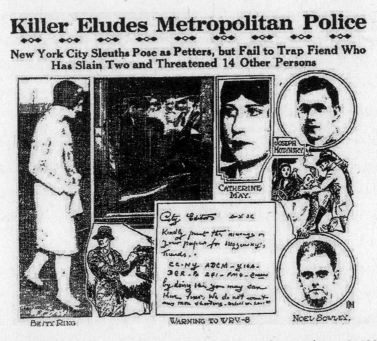

"Highlights in Mysterious 3X Murders" (*North Shore Daily Journal*, June 2, 1936.)

The newspapers continued their breathless coverage of the mysterious 3X murderer for months. Mae was just glad the department continued to keep her name out of the papers. She didn't need any more ribbing from her colleagues. Mae and other detectives on the squad continued to work the case for the next several months, but the trail was cold, dead cold. The case "is still one of the mysteries of the Queens Police Department. It has never been solved."[8]

Those young women who had been with their male companions when they were murdered eventually found their own ways back to normalcy. "With the 3X Murders passing day by day into the category of unsolved crimes, the two young women who were witnesses"[9] went back to work and back to their lives, but the notoriety of their status of victims stuck with them.

That fall, Mae decided she needed a break to take a trip, see some place new. She sailed to Germany with a few of her Broadway pals and saw the bustling city of Berlin, although the politics had a vibration that set her teeth on edge. It was a dangerous place, Mae thought. The Nazis were in charge and their movement was growing. It made her uneasy. She looked around each day and wondered how the average citizens could be so oblivious to the changes. Difficult times were coming.

In Germany, Mae took her first commercial airline flight, from Berlin to London. There she took in the changing of the guard at Buckingham Palace and saw a play, walked through Hyde Park, and drank a half pint of beer in a pub. Only ladies with shady reputations would order a whole pint at once, it seemed. Mae learned that tidy fact very quickly.

Finally, making up for the few years without a journey abroad, she traveled on to Egypt and took her second flight, this time down the Nile, viewing the pyramids from above and then atop a fairly uncooperative and definitely moody camel. She even rode that camel, although the smell didn't seem to leave her clothing or her suitcase for weeks. All too soon, the days of adventure ended, and she had to leave her fantasy life of wealth and luxury aboard the cruise ship where it belonged. It was time to return to reality and the job.

CHAPTER 9
RHYTHM AND BLUES

The Great Depression had an effect on hiring new policewomen, not only in New York but in police departments across the country. While fewer applied to join the NYPD, more female candidates did apply to take the civil service exam, the entry point to a government career. In many cases, the requirements for women were more detailed and exacting than the standards for men.[1] Yet it was a good time for men to don the uniform. Many highly qualified and talented young male applicants joined the NYPD, no doubt due to the difficulty in finding other employment.[2]

Writing in her autobiography in 1937, Mary Sullivan commented on the hiring trends during the Depression years. The number of male officers by then didn't reveal any increase at all; in fact, they had declined. The numbers of women hadn't increased much. "I wish that we were not so greatly handicapped in numbers," Mary wrote. "There are 18,000 men in the New York City Police Department, and only one hundred fifty women. Considering the immense number of cases that come our way, not a department in the municipal government is as badly understaffed."[3]

Mae was aware of these downward trends in hiring. She wasn't seeing that many women joining the force, and she was certain she hadn't gained any new policewomen as colleagues in the 108th or in the Policewomen's Endowment Association. But even as the country sank further into the Depression, she continued to be grateful for her job with the NYPD and the opportunities it provided her.

In 1931, her annual trip overseas took place in September. Three glorious weeks of sunshine and lavender fields in the South of France, and Mae was ready to return to New York. Or so she thought. Her ship sailed at the end of August from Cherbourg. On September 10, 1931, Mae stood at the rail on the top deck, looked up at the welcoming Statue of Liberty, and waved back at the grand dame while she breathed in the cacophony of noise and the melting pot scents from the global cultures that made her city home. It was good to be back.

Mae was still enjoying her new home in Queens. She started playing bunco with a group of ladies who belonged to the Alban Manor neighborhood Democratic Club. Bunco was like gambling, throwing dice and competing with other teams, but it wasn't really like gambling. After all, Mae assured herself, they may have thrown the dice, but no one was betting on the outcomes. But they sure counted up those points. The ladies who taught her the game were enthusiastic about it and looked forward to their meetings. It was a lively group, and with over fifty members, their bunco games were not just competitive, they were loud.

Basically the dice game is played with twelve players, at a minimum. They are divided into three tables with four players at each table. It didn't take Mae long to catch on to the game's goals, scoring points by rolling the number of the hand. For hand number three, for each die with the number three, one point would be scored. If all three dice match, it is called a bunco. Each game has six sets with six hands in each. Mae liked it that players rotated tables too. She usually got to chat with a number of ladies during each session that way.[4]

They met on the first Thursday of every month, sometimes for bunco tournaments at Almancia Hall, in the Jamaica neighborhood. Typically, little to no politics were ever discussed. It was more of a social club than an organizing or lobbying organization. Besides bunco, Mae enjoyed all the group's activities, from dinners to fancy hat parties, bus trips to museums. Even hayrides, although she was too much of a city girl to want to do that more than once.[5]

The Jamaica neighborhood was patrolled by officers from the 103rd Precinct. That meant Mae was a little farther afield from her own neighborhood, but there was less chance of someone recognizing her as a policewoman, questioning her about criminals, and saying the usual, "Oh my dear! How could you possibly do such a tough and violent job? What do all the men officers think?"

After all that "mercy me" fluttering, the really juicy questions would start. Even if the ladies tried to be delicate, Mae knew what they meant when they started in with, "Well, have you had any personal encounters with some of these mobsters we read about?" Or, "What do you know about so-and-so I just read about in the paper?"

Despite their breathless desire for salacious gossip, Mae disappointed them all, preferring to keep her business life and personal life separate. After the first few discussions, most didn't ask at all. Newcomers expressed the usual interest in her work after inquiring about her husband. Mae explained she was a widow and, to those who didn't know she was a police officer, answered any and all questions about her work by saying simply, "Oh, I just work for the city." They lost interest after that.

Some were a little bit more bold and enterprising, snapping open a large pocketbook to pull out a crumpled parking ticket and, with pleading eyes, asking Mae to fix it. Others complained about loud music being played by their neighbors or even a husband's minor brush with the law. "How was he supposed to know that was a tow-away zone?" one woman asked indignantly.

Mae answered every one of those pleas the same, saying simply, "Not in my jurisdiction, honey." That left her bunco teammates wondering. Maybe Mae could fix a ticket if she wanted to. Or maybe she could make the fine even higher.

Mae wasn't above being a bit mysterious. It was a skill she practiced on all her cruises to Europe. She was the mystery woman from Jackson Heights. She chuckled to herself every time she tossed the dice. And won. Mae usually won at bunco.[6]

Back at work, Mae kept her head down and did her job, but she was aware that the department was continuing to change around her. Constantly evolving, she thought. It almost made her think twice about her annual trips to Europe. Almost. But by the next fall, she was ready to go again and this time explored Paris and the north of France. There was a lot to think about on that trip. Her younger daughter, Grace, had gotten married in July at the age of twenty-three to a young man named Ted Mikridge. It was a whirlwind romance, and Mae had to remind herself to keep her mouth shut. Grace was head over heels, and when Ted got a job with a steam company, they moved to South Ozone Park in Queens.

Ted was a blond, blue-eyed boy with delicate features who had served as a seaman on merchant ships; Mae had misgivings about him from the beginning. After all, Ted had been an "ordinary seaman," working on freighters before finding a job to keep him in New York. She thought about those sailors she'd seen with the runaway girls during World War I and started to worry. Mae just shook her head. Grace was an adult, and this was who and what she wanted.

Florence was nowhere near ready to take the plunge. Mae didn't know which of them to worry about more, the staid older sister who wasn't even interested in going out to meet nice young men or young Grace, who grabbed the first good-looking man she could find and squeezed him tight. Mae didn't travel in 1933, saving her pennies for an exciting new opportunity: the NYPD promised a department-sponsored cruise around the world in 1934.

In 1933, the 108th Precinct commissioned a new group portrait of its officers. Mae had been with the 108th for three years by then, taken on hundreds of cases, and made more than her share of arrests. She was still the only woman in her precinct, but by God, she was front and center in that photo. By then, she was making $2,810.00 per year (equal to $59,804.09 in 2022) as a policewoman.[7] Less than a male officer, but she was still more than comfortable, particularly during the depths of the Depression. Mae smiled contentedly in her photo even as she tried her best to look tough.

These portraits were treasured mementos in the city's precincts and had been since the 1870s when the officers were gathered and stood together on the steps of their station house. By 1933, there were so many officers assigned that the photographers had to take individual portraits and create one large montage.[8]

The 108th Precinct in 1933. Note that the detectives were in plainclothes. Mae was the only woman in the precinct. (Photo courtesy of the Foley family.)

While Mae wasn't wearing a uniform because she was a detective, she actually didn't even have one to wear should she want to. However, in 1935, female officers were offered the opportunity and issued their own uniforms.

"Come on, Mom. I want to see you have a picture made with the uniform on," Grace said.

Florence agreed. "That's right. You look so tough in that blue suit. Why don't you hold up your gun like you're chasing a bad guy? That picture could deter crime all by itself!"

"You are a real comedienne, Flo," Mae replied drily. But she did finally give in and have her portrait taken in uniform. Mae gladly accepted the uniform for the recognition and respect it would grant on the street, but she hung on to the shield she had originally been issued. It was a big matter of pride to have a low number, and Officer #73 was definitely proud of her service.

Another new piece of equipment made its way into the hands of female police officers in 1933. Mae now had a very special new purse in shiny black leather outfitted with a tight little holster inside for her .38 revolver and even a slot for her lipstick, plus room for her powder and blush. *Everything a girl could possibly need*, Mae thought.

Carrying a service weapon was still voluntary for women in 1933, but a year later, it became mandatory to be armed on duty.[9] By 1934, annual training and practice with assigned weapons was also mandated, and Mae enjoyed regular pistol practice with her male colleagues. She was pretty good with the gun but was well aware her female colleagues were counting on it to stop crime more than they had before. During Mae's tenure, a number of senior women were demoted for public drunkenness or misuse of their service weapon. Others were fired or resigned. The more she heard those kind of stories, the more careful Mae became.

The 1934 department cruise around the world was more than a

once-in-a-lifetime adventure or even a luxurious vacation. It was school, and there was homework, which definitely took a toll on the enjoyment of evening activities aboard ship. The department held a full complement of training classes during sea days, and Mae took advantage of every single one offered. She also earned her colleagues' respect, if not amazement, when she claimed to be the first woman to ride a donkey along the trail to the Taj Mahal. And then she shared the pictures to prove it

As for crime itself? The Depression continued to accelerate its growth. By 1934, "there were seventy-five thousand homeless single women"[10] on the streets of New York. While men had shelters to go to, the women had no place to go, so they hid in train stations, rode the subways, or found ways to make a little money. Many turned to domestic work or even selling their bodies to get money for food. There were marches in the streets, women demanding jobs, seeking not just a way to get ahead but to survive. Many returned to school, took secretarial jobs, gave up on the vague dreams that lingered from the free-wheeling days of the Roaring Twenties.

The need for policewomen remained. In 1935, the department assigned four women officers to the Pickpocket Squad, including Irishwoman Mary Shanley. On her first day on the job, Mary arrested a suspect she saw opening and closing unwitting customers' pocketbooks at a department store counter. When the news of the arrest filtered back to the 108th's officers, Mae took a deep breath.

That used to be John's job, she thought.

"Deadshot Mary" Shanley continued on her brassy way, later chasing down two known criminals from a subway station up to Times Square and back again, firing her gun twice in the air to get them to stop.[11] Mary later said, "You have the gun to use and you may just as well use it."[12] She rose quickly in the department, getting results and enjoying the notoriety of her position.

She garnered over one thousand arrests of "shoplifters, confidence men, and pickpockets." By the time she was promoted to first-grade detective, she was known as a tough street cop. When she arrested a woman, she would typically say, "This is a pinch, honey." If it was a man, all she had to do was show her gun and let him know she knew how to use it.[13]

"Annie Oakley" they called her, and a host of other names besides. Mae thought waving a service weapon in the air and firing it just to get attention was more than melodramatic. Then she had a thought—maybe she was becoming a little stodgy, set in her ways. She asked the girls at their weekly dinner that night.

"So do you two think I'm a bit of a stick-in-the-mud?"

"Mom, why would you think that?" Grace plopped a spaghetti casserole on a potholder in the middle of the kitchen table. Ted was out with his friends playing cards. It was nice to have both girls over for dinner, Mae thought. Grace looked a big skittish though. Florence had dropped a pan on the floor, and while it made a loud bang, Grace had jumped as though she'd heard a bomb go off. Mae wondered why she was so jumpy.

"Well, things are changing in the department, and some of them seem a bit risky to me."

"You mean you aren't a showboat like old Deadshot Mary," Florence chimed in.

"Well, I'm a bit older than Miss Mary Shanley, thank you. You recall me telling you about Kitty Barry?"[14]

"What about her? She's a narcotics investigator, right?" Florence may not have looked like she was paying attention, but she never forgot a name.

"That's her. She has to keep her identity quiet. Otherwise she'd be compromised. I'm a lot like her. I just prefer to keep my name out of the papers."

"Good move, Mom. The department doesn't need another cowgirl," Florence added.

"Right, Mom. You wouldn't look good in the hat anyway." Grace added her two cents. "How about a glass of wine?"

"You know I don't drink!" Mae exclaimed. *Unless I'm on a cruise, that is.*

In 1933, Prohibition was repealed. *Good riddance*, Mae thought. The law had definitely caused more problems than it ever fixed. It transformed the city into a petri dish of violent crime that continued to evolve, grow, and impact every aspect of New York's culture. Mae thought the rise of organized crime was the worst outgrowth of Prohibition.

But then so was the police response. As criminals grew increasingly violent, the NYPD's response also grew in kind.[15] Mae knew all about "the third degree" and how many of her colleagues would attack suspects during questioning, beating them until they confessed. It was disturbing. That wasn't why she joined the force, and she didn't believe that was the role of police either.

But the aggressive approach continued through the Depression. In November 1934, when Fiorello La Guardia was mayor, then Police Commissioner Lewis Valentine grew frustrated with a series of unsolved shootings and urged police to "muss up" the gangsters. He argued that a hard line was necessary to curb crime and would eventually drive the criminals out of the city.[16]

But it didn't seem to be working. Obviously more than just the brutal use of fists and a nightstick was needed to deter organized crime. In 1935, Herbert H. Lehman, former partner in the Lehman Brothers financial investment firm and governor of New York, appointed Thomas Dewey as special prosecutor in the office of the Manhattan district attorney. Dewey had been a federal prosecutor, then worked in private practice. He made a name for himself getting convictions in several tough cases. But when the governor called, he snapped up the opportunity and the appointment. Dewey had political ambitions, and the chance to make his mark as tough on crime was too good to pass up. His new title: chief assistant U.S. attorney for the Southern District of New York. His charter: go after large-scale racketeering, the "numbers racket," gambling and prostitution rings, and the big-time gangsters.

He plunged right in, organizing his new office, hiring sixty assistant investigators, and petitioning the city for more help from law enforcement. Mayor La Guardia obliged and hand-picked sixty-three of the very best police officers available for an open-ended detail to Dewey's office.[17]

As Mae would soon learn, there was a good reason for Dewey's nickname, "Gangbuster."

CHAPTER 10
TRIALS AND TRIBULATIONS

"Do you know why the boss wants to see me?"

Eunice Carter, one of the prosecutors in Dewey's office, gave Mae a hooded look, then a quick nod. Her eyes darted back and forth, checking. She looked at the outside door, then locked it.

"Nobody's in here." Mae checked each of the stall doors there in the ladies' restroom. She and Eunice were alone. "Okay, tell me, Eunice."

Eunice was still checking the stalls.

"He's not going to send me back to the NYPD, is he?" Mae was getting used to how Dewey operated. It was a fast-paced job, but every investigation she had worked had been by the numbers—evidence meticulously gathered and maintained for trial, suspects and witnesses carefully interviewed and deposed. Cases were built without any notion of predetermined outcomes. When Dewey pronounced them ready for prosecution, they were ready for he and his staff to win.

Mae thought Dewey was one of the best bosses she'd had as a police officer, but she was deeply impressed with his assistant, a young African

American lawyer, Eunice Hunton Carter. Carter graduated cum laude from Smith College in 1921, and while working full-time in the Harlem Division of the Emergency Unemployment Relief Committee, she became the first Black woman to graduate from Fordham Law School in 1932. As the first Black and only female prosecutor in the Manhattan district attorney's office, she had to prove herself.[1] And she had.

"He wants to tell you himself, Mae," Eunice said in a near whisper.

"Oh, come on," Mae pleaded. "You know you can trust me. Just give me a hint."

"I do. I do trust you. Listen, I'll tell you this much. He's got a special assignment for you. And you're going to do just great. Now I've got to get back to work. You know that one case we've been working?"

Mae nodded. Everybody knew about that one case and Eunice's role in breaking it wide open.

"Just get ready. And don't say I didn't warn you." Eunice unlocked the bathroom door and slid out into the dark hallway and was gone.

Mae waited until she heard the clack of Eunice's heels fade away, then she checked her hair in the mirror, straightened her skirt, and headed into Dewey's outer office.

She sat there for a long twenty minutes, watching the clock on the wall and wondering why she had been summoned. Eunice passed by the door and their eyes locked. Mae looked away quickly. She had questions. A lot of questions she wanted answered.

Mae was in plainclothes, not required to wear a uniform since being seconded to the DA's office as a detective. When she was called in, she was surprised to see Dewey sitting at the conference table with a spreadsheet laid out in front of him. Ten minutes later, Mae left in a daze. Her new assignment was protecting the female witnesses in the trials of mobster Charles "Lucky"

Luciano and eight of his associates. That meant supervising all the patrolmen serving as escorts as well. No doubt that would prove more difficult than the witnesses themselves.

Mae knew that when Dewey was appointed as a special prosecutor for New York County (Manhattan), he took on a job that no one else wanted, but he believed it was his duty to restore law and order to the city, to go after the mobsters and get crime under control. His first target was Dutch Schultz, a mobster known for his ties to gambling and prostitution rings. Schultz heard from his informants that he was at the top of Dewey's hit parade; it wasn't a role he wanted. He went to visit crime boss Luciano and asked for permission to hire a gun to take down Dewey. Luciano refused, telling Schultz that murder was bad for business. Schultz then made a career-ending mistake. He decided to go ahead on his own, and word got back to the boss. Luciano wasn't to be ignored. He had Schultz killed for his disobedience, and the crime world learned that Luciano wasn't to be crossed.[2]

But in his show of power, Luciano had saved Dewey's life. And now Dewey turned his attention to Luciano's numerous criminal enterprises, estimated worth over twelve million dollars. Ultimately it was one of Luciano's minor business operations that broke apart and brought his entire operation to a standstill.

That success was due to Eunice Carter's insights and investigative ability. Her first job out of law school had been as a prosecutor in the so-called Women's Court, prosecuting female lawbreakers, including prostitutes. She knew the streets of New York, its politics, and in particular its bail bondsmen and "shyster" lawyers. When the DA's office turned its attention to Luciano's criminal businesses, among them was "the Combination"—a forced prostitution ring. Eunice began to dig into Luciano's employee records. Given her background, she quickly realized some interesting connections. The majority of the women arrested for prostitution across New York's five boroughs were represented by the same attorneys and bail bondsmen. Intrigued, Eunice continued digging. She next orchestrated synchronized raids of brothels, pulling in over one hundred prostitutes in one night.

Mae had worked the raids along with her colleagues and realized the sheer number of suspects was going to overwhelm the logistics of the syndicate's defenses. It was a brilliant approach. The accused streetwalkers couldn't get their attorneys to answer their calls or their bail bondsmen to have them released. There were too many suspects clamoring for attention at once. The resulting frustration led to many opting to talk to the police and the prosecutor's office, more than they would have thought possible. Mae smiled to herself. Eunice definitely knew how to turn the screw.

Piece by piece, Eunice assembled the puzzle, tying large numbers of prostitutes back to "the Boss," Luciano. By the time she had assembled enough evidence to have him arrested, Dewey decided to put another of his assistants in charge of the prosecution team. Attorney Barent Ten Eyck hadn't even been working the prostitution angle with Eunice. She was still working on the case, although relegated to the role of simply preparing evidence. She was pushed to the sidelines, something Mae had seen time and again during her work for the city.[3] When a woman succeeded at her job, she was often moved out, and someone else got the credit. Years later, Eunice spoke at a convention and commented, "Skill, talent, and ingenuity prevail in womankind as well as mankind."[4]

And all those traits were needed to manage a gaggle of prostitutes as prosecution witnesses, some willing but most not pleased with their role. Once the trial began on May 13, 1936, Mae quickly realized she had to do more than corral and manage the witnesses. That was a delicate and dangerous job itself, but she also had to worry about the potential for witness tampering, not to mention being concerned for their safety. By then, there were forty of them, female witnesses in what became known as Dewey's "parade of tarts."[5]

Originally the main witnesses were madams Florence "Cokey Flo" Brown, a seasoned longtime player with at least six aliases, and Mollie Leonard, plus twenty-seven other so-called working girls who agreed to testify. After a few weeks, Mae was no longer surprised when even more prostitutes were added to the witness list. Mae and a number of policemen and policewomen rode with the witnesses to court each day and took them back into protective custody in the evening, dropping them off at a safe house in the Jackson Heights neighborhood in Queens. At least there was one perk, Mae thought. Her home wasn't far away.

A group of female witnesses arrive at the Supreme Court, Manhattan, for court session. One of Mae's police escorts is leading the parade. Behind her is Betty Anderson, followed closely by Catherine O'Connor, who testified. (Photo by *New York Daily News* via Getty Images.)

Mae's job was all eyes and ears, surveilling the route to look for trouble, checking the witnesses for any attempts at communication with any of Luciano's associates or even attempted escapes, possible collusion of testimony, and more. She even had to check out how they were dressed for their appearances in court, making certain they were clean, modest looking, and presentable. But it was Luciano's criminal pals who worried her the most.

Despite the danger and multitude of risks, things seemed organized in the courtroom, although the tension continued to rise during the long days of testimony, objections, wrangling, and waiting. Always the waiting. To be called in the morning, waiting for the cars to come, delivering the women to court, waiting for them to finally leave the restrooms in the court building and head to their seats in the courtroom, repeating the whole hurry-up-and-wait routine at lunch and again once the day ended. Then to the cars again. Sleep, repeat.

Finally, things began to heat up. On May 19, thirty-seven-year-old Mollie Leonard, a.k.a. Mollie Glick, entered the witness box.[6] The *Long Island Daily Press* described her as a "dark, buxom madam of a disorderly house," a scowling woman with a hard look and a mean set to her shoulders, looking ready to point the finger. Mollie had been a streetwalker since the age of eighteen, and as a madam, she had long resented paying protection money to Luciano's organization to protect her girls. She directly linked "the Combination" to Luciano and pointed him out, the first time he had been so identified in court. Luciano glared at her while she testified, although he didn't say a word. His lawyers, though, popped up like marionettes and shouted objections, tossing papers into the air. Wide-eyed observers gasped and the courtroom stirred as reporters ran for the doors. Mae realized in that moment that the stakes had just gone up.[7]

It was dark when the day's session finally ended. "You're with me tonight," Mae said, crooking a finger. It had been a long day on those hard wooden benches in the courtroom, and Mae was ready to go home and put her feet up. She directed Mollie into her vehicle along with another two witnesses and a patrolman.

"I'll drive," Mae said. Backing out, she turned to look at her charges. "You'd better hang on," she said. "This could get interesting." The escorts were all well aware that Luciano's colleagues were eager to bump off as many of the witnesses as possible. As the trial continued, the threats increased. The witnesses gulped. Mollie had just moved up into first place on that list.

Mae was heading to the witness hideout in Jackson Heights when she noticed in the rearview mirror that her vehicle was being followed by another car, getting closer and closer to her rear bumper. She didn't say a word, didn't want any of the women turning around or starting to shriek. Mae increased her speed and shot a look at the policewoman in the back seat. The officer nodded in understanding.

Mae then hit the gas full out. She used her defensive driving and evasion tactics, weaving expertly in and out of traffic. She slowed down before a traffic light, then charged right through it just after it turned red. She gunned the engine down the street and cut in front of a taxi, whipping into a dark alley, cutting off all the lights. The witnesses were shocked for a moment, not moving, not breathing. Then Mollie started to cry and moan. "I shoulda never said nothing," she wheezed.

Mae held up a hand. *Be quiet.* "Shh," she added, watching out the back window as the chasing car sped harmlessly by. Mae kept them all in suspense for another few long moments before they continued on their journey, but instead of heading to the safe house, just in case it was compromised, she took her charges to another policewoman's home. She didn't sleep much that night, replaying the scene over again in her head.

She looked like she'd been on an all-night bender by the next morning. The district attorney summoned her from the courtroom, waving her into an unoccupied conference room down the hall. Hand on hips, a foot-tapping Dewey asked Mae why she hadn't gone on to the safe house as ordered.

Mae kept her cool. "We made it, Mr. Dewey. That's all that matters. That's why I'm here today," she explained. "You know what we're facing with this mob. If we hadn't made it, we would have all been machine gunned."[8] Matter-of-fact, Mae laid it out. She wasn't going to apologize.

Dewey nodded. He understood.

The guilty verdict was handed down on June 7, 1936. The courtroom was packed with police officers and onlookers, whispering excitedly to each other. Mae was standing in the back, her eyes not on the defendants as the verdicts were announced but on the female witnesses. Some looked relieved to be out of the courtroom. Most just seemed glad they were free and not about to be charged with prostitution.

Sentencing took place on June 18. One newspaper said, "Luciano took the blow without a show of emotion on his face, as gray as the rain-filled skies outside the courthouse."[9] Luciano and his codefendants received sentences of thirty to fifty years in prison.

Just two days after the trial ended, Patrolman George Heidt, one of the witness escorts, was out celebrating the verdict with a former star witness, both of them loud and intoxicated at a nightclub. Apparently, someone had time for more than escort duties during the trial, Mae thought. Police Commissioner Lewis Valentine had him removed from duty. No one was surprised.[10]

That investigation and trial had lasted a full year. Mae was certain the strain had shaved more than a mere year off her life. She decided she definitely needed a vacation, maybe a nice long trip to Italy, or perhaps the South of France. But that wasn't going to work out. Florence had just announced her engagement to a young man she'd started dating while Mae was distracted with the trial, Mr. Frederick Evans, a blond-haired, blue-eyed former sailor. By that time, Florence was thirty-two and clearly irked that it had taken her five long years to find a man following her younger sister's wedding. Florence had quit school after the eighth grade. Fred had completed the ninth. Their education levels were fairly typical of the times. According to U.S. Census records, in 1940, most young men had completed the equivalent of three years of high school.[11] Fred worked as a stock clerk at a shop in Queens, and Mae thought the two were a perfect match. Fred loved Florence's sense of humor and doted on her, rubbing her feet in the evening, hanging on her every word, laughing at all her jokes, no matter how sappy they were. For her part, Florence loved being adored. *Who wouldn't?* Mae thought.

Florence had never shown much interest in entering the police department, and Mae certainly didn't press either of her girls to consider it as an option. It was fine with Mae. She didn't need to talk much about her work when at home anyway.

Her eldest daughter's wedding took place on June 26, 1937, at their then local church, St. Joan of Arc, in Jackson Heights. Their pastor, Reverence T. J. Reilly, officiated. It was a major social event in the neighborhood. Over four hundred family and friends attended the nuptial mass, and as the *Elmhurst Daily Register* noted, the mother of the bride was "one of the most widely known policewomen in the city."[12] The reception was held at the Boulevard Tavern in Elmhurst, Queens. Mae had done her daughter proud, including her wedding gift of a three-week honeymoon in Bermuda.

Following the lengthy reception, Mae found herself getting a little weepy, wishing John were there to walk his daughter down the aisle and celebrate. Mae finally said goodbye to the last guests and hurried home. Then she shut the door and pushed the lock into place. She kicked off her high heels and breathed a sigh of relief. She carefully removed the receiver from the phone and set it on the floor. Then she placed a pillow over the dial tone's insistent buzz, the instrument demanding it be returned to active service.

A special treat was waiting; Mae had saved it for this exact moment. There it sat right in front of her in the living room, the wedding gift she'd bought just for herself, a brand-new Naugahyde recliner. She climbed on and cranked it back all the way, and with her feet up, she just lay still for a moment. Breathing in, breathing out. Her lips moved as she had a private conversation with John, telling him everything he had missed—how beautiful Florence looked, the dress, the friends who came, how his old buddies from Pinkerton still missed him. Eyes closed, she could feel herself drifting away. Finally, both of her girls were settled. Maybe now the pace of things would slow down a bit.

One sweltering afternoon, just a month after the trial's end, Mae decided to head to midtown, maybe do a little window shopping, treat herself to lunch, just relax a bit. She took the number 7 train to Grand Central. She exited onto Forty-Second Street and began to walk west, thinking she eventually she'd go west to Eighth Avenue and then head north for a few blocks to Madison Square Garden. The shops she was thinking about were on Fifth Avenue between Thirty-Fourth Street and Fifty-Seventh Street. But by then she was close to a major construction project. She was curious about the colossal site ahead, taking up all of the ground and the air between Fifth and Sixth Avenues. New York millionaire John D. Rockefeller Jr. was the financier who sponsored the project, acquiring the land from Columbia University.

The project encompassed nineteen buildings; Rockefeller Center would eventually cover twenty-two acres between Forty-Eighth and Fifty-First Streets. Mae was amazed to see how the project was coming along. Not only was it massive, but it was also beautiful, elegant, and futuristic.

Mae used her shield to gain access and strolled slowly through the newly completed underground mall complex. Workers were still applying the finishing touches to the soaring lighting and the inlaid tile floors. Mae skirted around them in the soft shadows. The building was the first to be air-conditioned in New York City, or at least it was the first Mae knew of, and she stared transfixed at the work ongoing on the art deco murals in the hallways and lobby while an icy breeze tickled the back of her sweating neck.

She took her time, seeing everything that she could possibly get close to, before reluctantly returning to the number 7 train and the trip back to Queens. The project would take another four years to complete, its dedication scheduled for November 1939. At the height of the Depression, the construction of Rockefeller Center employed over forty thousand people.[13]

Mae knew that her city was going to be all right.

CHAPTER 11
CHASING GOOD TIMES

"What do you think, Florence?" Mae unpacked the white marble tray she'd bought in Russia and held it out for her daughter to admire.

"It is beautiful, Mom. That white marble is so elegant. And oh my heavens to Betsy. It is heavy too!"

"I know, honey. The real thing. You won't believe what I had to do to get this out of Russia." Mae ran her finger along one of the gold veins in the marble.

"Mom, that had to be so dangerous. You shouldn't have taken a risk like that! I've read that no one is even allowed in to visit Russia now."

"Oh, it was worth it, let me tell you," Mae said. "Even if I did have to fool those damn communists."

"Mother! You will have to tell me everything," Florence replied. "I want to know that my mom isn't about to be arrested for causing an international incident."

"Not me, honey," Mae replied. "I just know when to show my shield, that's all. It works every time."

In 1938, the NYPD held its first civil service exam for those women who wanted to earn a policewoman's shield. While about eleven thousand applied to take the exam, only about five thousand women actually sat the test, hoping for a place in the next class of police officers. Over three hundred passed. Among those women who passed the exam were a doctor, a journalist, and a private investigator. It took another year for twenty of those who passed the test to enter the police academy. When they were finally sworn in, their starting salary was about $2,000 a year.[1]

Mae's salary was nearly twice that by the time the exams began, and she'd been looking forward to traveling again since before the Luciano trial. It was a sultry June morning when Florence dropped her off at the cruise ship dock at New York Harbor. Mae didn't even look back at her daughter to wave goodbye. She was practically running for the gangway even though she was early to board.

The elegant cruise liner MS *Kungsholm* was bound for Gothenburg, Sweden. Part of the "White Viking Fleet," so named because of their white-painted hulls instead of the traditional black, the elegant ship held a hint of promise for Mae, something new, exciting, and a little bit mysterious. She stood at the rail as the ship pulled out from the New York Harbor and smiled to herself.

The first port, though, was something of a surprise. The flagship of the Swedish American Line headed straight for Wilmington, Delaware, where the ship's VIP passengers, Sweden's crown prince Gustaf Adolf and crown princess Louise, took part in ceremonies honoring the three hundredth anniversary of Sweden's landing in America in 1638. Mae watched with a bemused smile at the pomp and circumstance of the day's events. She was ready to travel onward, so much so that she thought of offering to help raise the anchor herself. Finally, with a last ceremonious blast of her horn, the *Kungsholm* pointed east and headed out to sea.[2]

What lay ahead was four full weeks away, including travel time plus sixteen days of adventure, plus a visit to the new Russia, post-revolution. On board ship, she ran into several old friends from Broadway. There was stage actress Dorothy Stickney, her husband, actor/playwright Howard Lindsay, and close friends Russel and Alison Crouse. In her autobiography, *Openings and Closings*, Dorothy recalled that they shouldn't have taken the trip at all. Unlike Mae, her stage friends were nearly broke, but they decided to go anyway. They needed a grand trip, actually a major distraction from their failure to launch a successful play, and this was it.

"We spent a day each in Norway, Sweden, Denmark, Iceland, and Finland and loved them all. Then we went to Russia, starry-eyed and open-armed, to see what this wonderful new Russia was like since the Revolution,"[3] Dorothy recalled.

What they found was that it wasn't that wonderful after all. It wasn't even that it was drab and gray, cold skies and even colder Russian people on the streets. All the passengers had to fight to get visas to travel to Moscow. In total, the friends spent three days in Russia. Later in her memoir, Dorothy said, "The Russians made it very plain that they didn't want us—in fact ours was the last cruise ship allowed in before the Iron Curtain fell."[4] They were watched, escorted, and followed throughout their trip. A visit to the former palace of the czar was intended as a propaganda showpiece for the new state. All it did, in fact, was make the visitors feel sorry for the former royal family and their passing.

Once back in Leningrad, the friends were ready to board the ship when they learned that Soviet rules forbade taking anything of value out of the country. Mae's stage friends were frustrated they were forced to leave their hard-won souvenirs behind. Yet all Mae had to do was flash her NYPD badge and she waltzed past the Russian customs officials with a beautiful marble tray under her arm. That was an unforgettable moment for Mae.[5] She held up her prize like a prizefighter winning the heavyweight belt. But once back on board, her triumph was short-lived. She was nearly knocked to the deck while carrying the tray back to her cabin.

Dorothy commented, "When we sailed out of port the ship suddenly listed far to one side. Everyone ran to the deck to see why. A Russian destroyer had suddenly cut across our bow in a gesture that said plainly: 'We are powerful here, so don't fool with us—just get out.'"[6]

Mae was shaken too. What she had seen of the repressive inner workings of communism left her with a sense of unease about the future of U.S. relations with the Soviet Union. She saw communism as a serious threat. "Half the people don't understand what it really means," she would say.[7] But no one was interested in her thoughts on Russia. Not yet anyway.

Once home, the full realization of what she'd seen in Russia hit her full force. While she showed the marble tray to Florence and tried to minimize the danger they'd all faced in Leningrad, Mae didn't talk about it for years, not until well after World War II.

Her friends went back to doing what they did best, the theater. It would be another year before Howard and Russel's new play *Life with Father* opened at the Empire Theatre on November 8, 1939. Mae was on hand for the event, planting herself right in the front row, center stage. That show made the playwrights and actors rich. From the days when she was worried about how they would pay for that cruise to Scandinavia, Dorothy became known as one of the grand leading ladies of the theater. *Life with Father* ran for a record-setting 3,224 performances, over four hundred weeks, becoming the longest running nonmusical play in Broadway history, a record that still stands. It spawned a movie featuring Elizabeth Taylor and later a television series.

Mae's playbill from *Life with Father*. (The Playbill, New York Theatre Program Corporation, 1942.)

For twenty-eight years, Lindsay and Crouse collaborated on numerous hits, garnering a Tony Award in 1960 for their musical, *Cinderella*. But their biggest hit was the unforgettable story of love and war, *The Sound of Music*, a testament to their friendship, creative talents, and gift for storytelling.[8]

Mae would tell anyone who would listen that she knew these stars when they were still struggling unknowns, way back when. But in those first days back on the job at the district attorney's office, no one wanted to listen to her vacation adventure stories. Another trial was coming. Another important one.

Mae got the news she'd been dreading. The saying at the station house was a caustic view of success. As the other detectives told her, "You know how it goes, Mae. No good deed goes unpunished."

Because of her skills in managing disreputable women by the dozen in the last major trial, Mae was given the same assignment as before. She was in charge of escorting the material witnesses to and from the trial each day. The only difference was the location of the safe house, this time in Long Island City.

Mae was glad she'd taken her annual vacation early this year. If she'd waited, there was no doubt she'd have had to change her plans due to the whims of the court, the jury, the witnesses, and particularly her boss. Everything including the weather could have blown her off course. No, she'd made the right choice.

District Attorney Thomas Dewey understood Mae's love of travel and its ability to absorb the mind enough to forget the stress of the job. His getaway was a huge farm he named Dapplemere, near Pawling, sixty-five miles north of New York City. He only got there on weekends if he was lucky, but on some occasions, it was almost enough just to know the farm was there waiting.

Following the conviction of Lucky Luciano, Dewey amassed an incredible record of seventy-two convictions out of seventy-three prosecutions. By 1938, the rising star was thinking about new opportunities even as he continued to prosecute criminals. He held daily briefings so he could keep up with the fifteen or so felony investigations his staff of attorneys, police detectives, and civilian investigators were working on. Dewey was an outstanding administrator and boss. He reorganized the DA's office and developed the infrastructure necessary to enable success, creating bureaus for fraud, racketeering, and juvenile crime. He hired and kept talent, maintaining his reputation for honesty and conducting investigations with a level of zeal that matched his integrity.

But his focus was also on his career and carving out a path to move ahead. By the summer, Dewey was on the public's pedestal as a genuine American hero. A Gallup poll showed over 3 percent of his fellow Republicans backed him as their choice for the 1940 presidential nomination.[9] Movies were made about his success, and he wasn't immune to the attention. He complained to friends while on vacation in June that "in five days only one person" had asked for his autograph.[10]

But first, he had to get through this major trial and win. The subject of the prosecution was politician James "Jimmy" Hines. Mae thought if Dewey could pull this one off, he was a sure bet to make it to the governor's mansion or the White House. Not that he condoned betting, of course.

The Jimmy Hines trial brought more corruption out into the open. Hines was accused of violating lottery laws, and besides complicity in the numbers game, he was also accused of providing protection for the now deceased Dutch Schultz. Dewey ran the prosecution like he had so many others, but in this case, he ran afoul of the judge. On September 12, 1938, the judge declared a mistrial, and Jimmy Hines walked free. Dewey was shocked, but more than his surprise at the outcome, he was worried the case would affect his future in politics. It did.[11] Dewey ran for governor that fall and lost. But he wasn't the kind of man to give up, either in politics or in his belief in his ability to do the right thing and make it count.

By the time of the retrial, Mae had moved on from her special assignment. When Police Commissioner Lewis Valentine released his 1938 holiday message to the force in December, Mae was enjoying the daily routine of a policewoman once again. Valentine's words held special meaning for her that Christmas: "Let us continue to render that patient and courteous service that is so essential if we are to merit the confidence, cooperation, and good will of our people."[12]

Mae was just glad to have returned to the 108th Precinct and her regular job. Too much politics, too much visibility in her court-supporting roles. She'd been with the DA's office for two plus years by then, and it was all theatrics, she thought. She preferred her drama in the actual theater. It was as one of the reviewers said of *Life with Father*: "For the theater is concrete, vivid, and magnetic. When it says something well, it leaves an indelible mark."[13] And that wasn't just posturing.

Plus, a play had a beginning and an end. Once the curtain closed in the theater, the play was finished. Mae hoped she wouldn't be called on again.

Even regular old crime seemed refreshing after those long days sitting on hard wooden benches in the Hines trial courtroom and trying to stay awake as lawyers bickered in their legalese. She enjoyed being back in action again, having the opportunity to get out into the community and do some good.

Thomas Dewey was later elected governor of New York, in both 1942 and 1946, and he continued to do good on behalf of the people of New York. Eunice Carter, his former assistant prosecutor, campaigned for him, bringing out the Black vote. In 1944, he ran unsuccessfully for president, losing to Franklin D. Roosevelt. In 1948, he lost again, forever memorialized in the photo of President-Elect Harry Truman holding up the newspaper with the headline "Dewey Wins."

CHAPTER 12

UNDERCOVER AND
OUT OF SIGHT

"Mom, Fred and I are going to the World's Fair this weekend. Why don't you come with us?"

"I can't, Flo. You know I can't." Mae sighed.

"Oh, please, Mother. It's not like anyone is going to recognize you." Florence plopped down on the sofa in Mae's living room. She usually visited on Sunday afternoons. Grace came on Saturdays. Mae didn't want to ask why they couldn't come together.

"I can't take the chance, Florence, I'm undercover. You know what that means. Maybe next spring, when the fair starts up again, we can all go."

"All right. Suit yourself. But you're going to be sorry. I heard there are televisions all over the grounds and the views of the future are just spectacular. I really want to see what's new in the food pavilions, and Fred is excited to check out what they have in the transportation section."

"I guess you'll just have to come back with some really great stories for me," Mae said. "And a box of saltwater taffy, please." She really wanted to go. But it wasn't a good idea. She didn't need to be out in public in a different role than the one she was playing. Besides, what if she inadvertently exposed Florence and Fred to danger just by being seen with her? No, Mae couldn't risk it.

Millions of visitors flocked to New York in 1939 to attend the World's Fair in Flushing Meadows, Queens. The theme of the fair was "Building the World of Tomorrow." Mae thought it was a more accurate title than the organizers probably realized, since the site of the fair was on an ash dump. But that was the only site available. When there wasn't any large plot of land free in Manhattan or Brooklyn, Queens offered up their dump.

The fair itself was meant to establish a firm note of hope, emerging from the Depression and looking ahead to a new age of prosperity and success.[1] President Roosevelt gave the opening day speech and set the tone for the magnificent new world to come. He said, "We Americans offer up a silent prayer that on the continent of Europe from which the American hemisphere was principally colonized, the years to come will break down many barriers to intercourse between nations, barriers which may be historic but which also have through the centuries led to strife." It was a prescient speech that fully predicted the war years that lay ahead and the peace that lay far beyond it. The world of the future lay in the 1960s, the fair declared, and at the time that was a heady promise.

The president concluded his speech by saying, "The time has come for me to announce, with solemnity but also with great happiness...that I dedicate the World's Fair, the New York World's Fair of 1939 and I declare it open for all mankind."[2]

The president's speech was the first scheduled live broadcast in the United States but available only to those within a twenty-five-mile radius of the fair itself, because the signal could only reach so far. Mae didn't have a television then. Only about one thousand New Yorkers did. The wooden box with the tiny screen was terrifically expensive then, costing what would equal about $4,000 today. Mae could definitely do without that.

But as she'd told her daughter, Mae would have to wait to see the fair in person. By the fall of 1938, she was back from her assignment with the DA's office and hand-picked for a very different type of assignment. This time, she would be going undercover in what could potentially be a long-term and dangerous situation.

She was so deeply entrenched in her undercover work that even her shield, her prized possession that she never liked to part with, even abroad, was at home, tucked away in a drawer. Her uniform hung in the closet, policewoman purse on the floor, service revolver in the little safe under her bed. And Mae couldn't go near any police station, much less her own precinct. Instead, she frequented the regular meetings of the German American Bund, an American Nazi organization, watching and pretending to eagerly listen to what the organizers were planning, trying to break deeper and deeper into their ranks.

Throughout the Depression, members of the German American Bund paraded through New York in their brown shirts with the swastika armbands, crying out "Heil Hitler!" and at times escalating to the point of accosting Jewish citizens on the street. A similar group was the popular Christian Front; one survey pegged at least four hundred NYPD serving officers as registered members. By 1938, the department began to employ more plainclothes detectives to infiltrate the organizations, to conduct surveillance and collect intelligence. This approach was part of a major policy change, away from head-cracking confrontations in the street and focused instead on tracking potential criminals and preventing violence.[3]

Mae kept up with the meetings, the fiery speeches, the braggadocio, and the propaganda about the Bund's plans for a new world to come. She gathered intelligence about their events, summer camps, parades, and rallies and made regular reports. But once past the holidays and into the dull winter days of January 1939, she was ready for the whole assignment to end.

The speeches were simplistic and repetitive, the members shallow and easily duped. Mae found herself becoming bored with the meetings. The leaders were childish and narcissistic, she thought. Mae made her reports though, dutifully mailing them to her bosses back at the precinct and calling in at least weekly for questions, always ready to warn the force if it appeared something major was about to happen. She knew there were undoubtedly other detectives undercover as well, but she didn't want to know who or where. They didn't need to meet.

It was exhausting, more than Mae could even admit to herself. Even if she could have gone to the World's Fair with Florence and Fred, she probably wouldn't have had the energy to walk the length of the fairgrounds. Nazi songs haunted her sleep. At least she didn't have to think about a German pavilion at the fair. Nazi Germany had pulled out at the last minute.

Keeping up with the meetings and memorizing faces and names of the Bund's many subgroups and officers was difficult enough. She also had to fend off advances from some of the more forward brown-shirted men, who found the nice widow attractive. It was all Mae could do to keep herself from using her jujitsu moves on them. She was constantly on guard, on alert, ready to fend off any untoward comments or accusations. If the gassy, pouting music from the Bund's oompah band invaded her dreams, she would startle awake, then be unable to sleep again. She lay awake worrying about the country, the city, and her family. But it was important work. Necessary. And she kept at it, even as her feet dragged and her eyes drooped.

When the Bund announced plans for a rally, Mae bought her ticket along with thousands more of the faithful. It cost a dollar and ten cents for a seat on the floor of Madison Square Garden.[4] Mae hoped she would be back far enough in the crowd to not have to see the events unfold up close.

That was why she was surprised when the captain called her first. Of course, she knew the NYPD would have to be out in force if the Bund was planning a big rally. The city had to be ready for violence or counterprotests. The purpose of the rally was supposedly a celebration for President George Washington's birthday. At least that was what they called it; Mae suspected it was going to be a lot more than that. But going into the event, Mae had no idea how big this supposed rally was actually going to be.

"Be careful, Mae," her captain warned her. "First sign of trouble, you get out."

"But, sir!" Mae protested, as he should know she could handle herself.

"No, Mae. You can't help with this. You're going to be in the crowd as one of them. You'll be seen as a Nazi just like the rest. There might not even be time to get out, much less let your fellow officers know you're there. Mayor La Guardia is really concerned. We're already on alert. All precincts are involved. You understand?"

"Yes, sir," she said reluctantly. "All hands on deck." Mae was on the wrong side of the fence on this one. And she didn't like it. Not at all.

"Be careful, Mae. Don't take any chances."

"I will. I'll find a way." Even if it meant hiding out under the stage all night long, Mae would keep out of the fray. She wasn't about to be caught between the two sides.

As wispy flakes of snow fell on Manhattan the night of February 20, 1939, Mae pulled her tan coat with the fake fox collar up around her neck and walked up the steps from the subway at Times Square. She hustled through her old neighborhood, down Eighth Avenue toward Eighth and Forty-Ninth Street, where the Garden was then located.

It was chilly, but Mae was reluctant to get to the arena and the rally itself. She found her steps slowing as she drew closer. Finally, Mae shook herself and took a turn, just a little detour through her old neighborhood, reminding herself of earlier good times and promising herself they would return again. She even backtracked a bit, taking her time strolling down East Thirty-Seventh Street by the stately Union League Club. Mae liked the look of the elegant private club; some of her society friends belonged. But not her and especially not then. She peered at the warm lights inside and sighed; she had to stick to her mission.

There were twenty-two thousand of the faithful there that night, showing their allegiance to the Bund, the Nazi Party, and to Adolf Hitler himself. Not George Washington, birthday or not. Mae was wedged in with the lot of them, feeling her arm tingle in stiff resistance as it did every time she had to stretch it out in the formal Nazi salute.

The bodyguards paraded in first in perfect unison, marching crisply with their set faces and stiff limbs. The drums followed, loud and commanding attention. On either side of the dais were men in uniform, holding large banners with gigantic swastikas emblazoned on them. The rallying cry started off the evening with thunderous echoes of "Free America! Free America! Free America!"[5] Even as the very floor shook with the power of that chant, Mae felt the bile rise in her throat as she forced a smile and a weak cheer.

Mae's view of the stage at Madison Square Garden. With storm troopers filling
the aisles, the crowd sang "The Star-Spangled Banner." This was the opening
of the German American Bund's Americanization Rally on February 20, 1939.
(Photo by Larry Froeber/NY Daily News Archive via Getty Images.)

Then there were the interminable speeches, one after another. The band played heavy oompah music. Finally, the leader of the German American Bund himself stepped up to the podium. Fritz Kuhn was flanked by swastikas, American flags, and a gigantic portrait of George Washington. Mae's lip curled up in a tight smile; it was all she could do to not gag at the juxtaposition of ideologies.

Kuhn was decked out in his dress uniform, large belly restrained by the Sam Browne belt. Once a criminal in the German Fatherland, he'd immigrated to America and taken advantage of her opportunities, managing to find a good job as a chemist. But Kuhn was a charismatic speaker and leader. He built a movement based on the Aryan ideals espoused by the Nazi Party in Germany, and as membership grew, he assumed the title of Bundesführer. He took his time gazing about the packed arena, drinking in the power of the moment.[6]

"We, with American ideals, demand that our government be returned to the people who founded it,"[7] Kuhn thundered, his voice echoing through the crowd. Mae held her breath and wished she could plug up her ears. He continued to speak for another long forty-five minutes. Finally with a flourish, the meeting dragged to a conclusion.

Mae's fingers shook as she buttoned her coat up tightly and tied a scarf about her neck. Then, head down, she trotted back toward the subway at Times Square. No delays on the way back. She wanted to get home. It was only a short hop back to Jackson Heights, but tonight it felt as though she had been transported to Germany itself and home was a long way off. There were over seventeen hundred police officers on duty outside the Garden, ready for trouble and hoping it wouldn't come. Mae didn't look up at them. She walked down the line of blue, hoping the officers wouldn't recognize her. Then she heard a voice she recognized, an Irish patrolman she knew from the 108th.

"Ah, Christ. Not you, Mae. Not you." The brogue was thick and coated with a heavy layer of disgust.

Mae stiffened and hurried on, tears hot against the snowflakes on her cheeks. *No, not me,* she thought. *They should know I'm undercover.*

Once she'd elbowed her way onto the train, she slumped against a window and took a deep breath, thankful the night ended peacefully. The next day, she learned only thirteen arrests had been made, all for minor infractions.[8] It was a blessing. Things could have easily gone the other way and turned into a riot.

That rally was actually the high point for the Bund in New York. Afterward, membership began to fall off and interest faded, helped along by the May release of the movie *Confessions of a Nazi Spy.* In the summer of 1939, the district attorney's office launched an investigation into the Bund's finances, revealing that Kuhn had been embezzling money from the organization to support his mistress, nearly $14,000 worth.

Just like Lucky Luciano, Mae thought. It was always the little things that tripped them up.

Even though Mae was technically still undercover following the Bund's big rally, she missed regular police work. She was permitted to resume limited detective duties while remaining on call if needed for depositions or testimony in the Kuhn trial.

In April 1939, just after declining Florence's invitation to the World's Fair, Mae and Detective Edward Hatrick responded to a call about a theft of $220 from a woman's purse. The victim had been enjoying a nice dinner with her husband at a diner on Queens Boulevard in Forest Hills when she accidentally left her purse behind on a chair. She remembered it as soon as they reached the parking lot and rushed back in only to find it missing. Mae searched the main suspect, a waitress named Sally Dufresne, and found seventy dollars secreted on her person. While the woman protested that the stash was all tip money, Mae wasn't buying it. Otherwise, the bills wouldn't have been tucked into her bra; they would have been resting in the communal tip jar at the back of the kitchen.

Sally cried and lied, but in the end, she was charged with theft. They turned the sullen woman over to two patrolmen to be booked. Mae liked it when there was a quick resolution to an issue and justice was done.[9] Or at the very least on its way to being done.

On the way back to the station house, she thought about how throughout her career, she'd been asked to do things that the men either couldn't or wouldn't do. Search female suspects like Sally, or like Isabella Goodwin twenty plus years earlier, go undercover and seek out evidence of criminal behavior. Sure, Isabella thought women made good storytellers and actresses. Mary Sullivan said the same thing. But Mae realized there was another side to that coin.

Women were successful in their roles as policewomen, detectives, and even prosecutors because society held them in such low regard that they were above suspicion when it came to planning any operation or seeking out information. Who could think a woman was capable of doing such things?

Mae turned to her partner. "Ed, let me ask you a question. How would you have handled Sally back there if I wasn't with you?"

"Aw, I don't know, Mae. I would have probably asked the same questions you did."

"And when she broke down and cried?"

He shrugged. "I'd just cuff her and haul her out of the diner and into a patrol car."

"And if she resisted?" Mae watched his hands grip the wheel.

"Well, she wouldn't resist for long, let me tell you." His jaw was set.

"That's what I thought," Mae replied.

Another reason policewomen were critical to law enforcement, Mae thought. They got results quickly, kept situations from escalating into violent confrontations, and actually talked to suspects like they were human beings. Coercion wasn't necessary in Sally's case. Probably not in hundreds of others either.

Although there was very little happening with her undercover assignment, Mae continued to be listed on the books as part of the Bund investigation. That summer, she read an article in the paper about the exploits of one Mary Shanley, now a detective first grade with the Pickpocket Squad. There were six other women on the squad by then, but with her $4,000 annual salary, Shanley claimed to be the highest paid woman "in active service as a detective on the New York Police Force."[10]

Mae smiled to herself. Her work was considerably more dangerous than traipsing around after purse snatchers and chair tippers after all. But she didn't say a word. She was still playing a role. She didn't need to.

By the fall, Dewey issued an indictment, and Fritz Kuhn was put on trial in November 1939. In a surprise move, the defense called Dewey as a witness. Kuhn's attorney baited him with a question about his personal dislike of the Bund leader. Dewey responded coolly, "I should say that never having seen the man I have no personal feelings—but I regarded him as a menace to the community and probably a threat to civil liberties."[11]

That did it. Kuhn was found guilty on December 6 and was sentenced to two to five years in Sing Sing Correctional Facility.[12] Mae was finally released from her undercover assignment and was delighted to spend the holidays at home. She was more than happy to trash that swastika armband and put the Nazis and their propaganda behind her.

The NYPD liked to hold their major ceremonies at large public venues. In June 1940, the commissioner felt it sent a message that the department was growing, becoming more modern, well trained, and prepared to serve the citizens of New York. He scheduled the swearing-in ceremony for the NYPD class of 1940 on the grounds of the Court of Peace at the World's Fair. That visit was Mae's only trip to the fair grounds. The view of the "World of Tomorrow" in 1940 was vastly different from that vision as portrayed just a year earlier. The pavilion for Poland was dark, the country having been invaded by both Germany and Russia, yet the Russian pavilion continued to attract visitors. It occupied a prime location at the fair. The pavilions for Italy and Japan were still open as well, but Mae avoided them.

But she was able to speak with another former colleague there that day. Henrietta Additon had established the Crime Prevention Bureau for the NYPD, the forerunner of the Juvenile Aid Bureau. In 1937, the city appointed her to head up the Welfare Unit for the World's Fair. Her credentials were extensive: "An authority on community planning, social work, problems of childcare, juvenile delinquency, and crime prevention."[13] She was a perfect choice to look out for the need of thousands of young people attending the fair, Mae thought. Later, she would continue to serve, although in a different capacity: corrections. Henrietta was named superintendent of Westfield State Farm, a women's correctional facility, where she concentrated on rehabilita- tion.[14] Mae admired her dedication and was impressed by the new graduates, young policewomen working to keep the fair safe for everyone in attendance.

Just a month later, the World's Fair was the site of a bombing, in a case that was never solved. On the Fourth of July, two months into the fair season, a device was found at the British Pavilion in the International Zone. A display of captured Nazi contraband was a popular attraction there, and the police had been receiving threatening calls from anonymous men with German accents. Bomb Squad detectives Joseph Lynch and Ferdinand Socha responded to the bomb threat. They confronted a ticking attaché case with only a pocketknife and pair of pliers. Lynch cut the case open with his pocketknife and looked up at his colleague. "It's the business," he said.[15] Before either could utter another word, the bomb went off. The detectives were killed instantly, the massive detonation carving a hole in the grounds over six feet wide and three feet deep. Thousands of German American Bund members were rounded up and questioned, but the perpetrators were never located.[16]

The disaster led to changes in how the Bomb Squad operated in the city, and innovations in protective gear were added. A new vehicle was developed to use in safely disposing of bombs.[17] It was actually the mayor's idea. Mayor Fiorello La Guardia wanted a huge truck that could safely haul unexploded bombs away to isolated spots for detonation. Thinking about his officers who had died in the blast, Lieutenant James Pyke, commander of the Bomb Squad at the time, went to work on the design, perfecting it in the NYPD's technical laboratory. Tests showed the massive truck worked as designed and could withstand a blast of up to twenty-four sticks of dynamite. The La Guardia-Pyke Bomb Carrier, which resembled a pioneer covered wagon, was quickly adopted by the department. The GM truck pulled a trailer carrying a steel mesh cage with the word DANGER emblazoned on all sides. The heavy cage was designed to capture shrapnel or debris if the bomb detonated prematurely. A version of the La Guardia-Pyke truck was still use in the 1990s.[18]

The world was becoming a more dangerous place, Mae thought, but she wanted to see it all. And she definitely needed to get away. Europe was out of the question. War was breaking out as Germany was continuing to invade and declare war on its neighbors, but that wasn't going to stop Mae from her escape.

She pulled out her torn and dog-eared old travel map from the bookcase, spreading it out on her dining room table, marked with red dots to signify all the places she'd been. Behind her, the overstuffed china cabinet held treasures from all her previous travels. She took a moment to glance at the Delft vases from Amsterdam, the little British flag, Hummel figurines from Germany, a photograph of herself atop a camel at the Great Pyramids, a painted mug from Italy, a fading bundle of French lavender, and the big prize, that heavy marble tray from Russia.

Maybe something new this time, as different as it could be. She put a question mark on the route to Alaska and drew a wide red circle around the circumference of Central America. Those two vastly different regions would both be contenders for next trips. In between more undercover assignments, at least.

Finally, by September 1940, she managed a terribly short two weeks away on a cruise from Seattle up to Alaska. The Inside Passage was lovely, the people watching as entertaining as ever, and the smoked salmon divine, but there was one major disappointment. The northern lights eluded her, but as she told one of her traveling companions, she never gave up. One way or another, sooner or later, the clouds would part and the aurora borealis would appear in the night sky, just as she had planned it would.

As always, the trip with its long lazy days and deeply restful nights was over too soon. It was time to return to New York, this time by train from the West Coast, and climb back into her role as respected policewoman, upholder of the law, and manager of order. Time to learn her next assignment and see what strange treasures it would hold. Undercover again? Undoubtedly.

After all, who would ever suspect a middle-aged woman of being a spy? Well, most never suspected she could be a detective either. She wondered what the future held: years of ferreting out German saboteurs, infiltrating an espionage ring, and having to uncover acts of sabotage or even potential war crimes. It seemed infinitely more stressful than it was to work in law enforcement during World War I and definitely more dangerous than dealing with plain old murderers, thieves, and con artists, that was certain. It took her work to a whole new level, a level where politics and international relations were at play. Mae just wanted to travel, not worry about how global events were going to change her life. But they were.

CHAPTER 13

WAR AGAIN

In July 1941, Mae turned fifty-three, with eighteen years of service as a sworn officer, and still, no one day on the job was like any other. It was the variety Mae liked. There was definitely an element of surprise in each case, a life lesson in values or the dangers of guesswork, the satisfaction in getting justice for a victim, the pride in keeping the city safe for its citizens, particularly young women and girls.

But there was one chore she personally detested, and that was the special task all policewomen got to experience at one time or another. Mae had more practice than most, having been called on hundreds of times over the years to search the bodies of female DOAs. Dead on arrival, the victims were deceased, whether due to "suicides, homicides, or merely a case of suspicious circumstances,"[1] it didn't matter. If it happened in the 108th Precinct, Mae got the call. She'd learned that she needed to move fast, get on-site before the coroner's van arrived, and then thoroughly conduct her inspection, search the body, and examine the surrounding area.

Mae's nearly two decades on the force, her keen eye for critical details, and her insights into potential affecting circumstances often led to deductions that proved essential to an investigation. She knew detectives and a bevy of young patrolmen would be waiting, pens out, notebooks at the ready, to hear her insights. She would do her work in silence as they watched, then provide relevant information to the detectives on-site. They knew they could proceed with confidence that Detective Mae Foley had set them on the right path to determine what had happened and who was responsible.

By the early 1940s, there were more women coming into the force, and Mae was instrumental in giving them the benefit of her expertise. One of the new officers was Gertrude "Gertie" Schimmel. Outspoken, loud, and often profane, she became known as the Ethel Merman of the NYPD, but her career laid the groundwork for women to finally gain the right to go on street patrols and into squad cars.[2]

Gertie sat the police exam in 1939, but while she was third on the order of merit list, she wasn't yet twenty-one, so she was skipped over for that class. She entered the academy along with seventeen other women and three hundred men in what became known as the famous class of 1940. This first post-Depression class contained over two hundred college graduates and produced a police commissioner, a chief inspector (equivalent to today's chief of department), and dozens of captains and higher. Only six of the three hundred remained at the rank of patrolman throughout their service.[3]

Gertie went on to have a groundbreaking career. In 1962, she and another policewoman, Felicia Shpritzer, took the exam for promotion to sergeant. While they had the two highest scores on the test, the department insisted that women weren't physically able to "handle advanced jobs" and refused to promote them. The women sued, and they were promoted in 1965, although the New York Times was quick to point out that "no policeman will be supervised by a woman."[4]

Gertie ignored the media and her critics and continued to challenge the brass ceiling. In 1971, she became the NYPD's first female captain. By 1974, she was a deputy inspector. Her trailblazing efforts led to more changes in policing.[5]

The notion of men and women together in patrol cars sparked protests, not just by the male officers but by their spouses. The wives marched from police headquarters to city hall, loudly voicing their objections to the media. The newly elected president of the Patrolmen's Benevolent Association said he would "press for the removal of women from foot and automobile patrol because they lacked the physical and emotional ability to handle violent situations." Gertie adroitly dismissed their arguments. "Nothing is factual, it's all emotional," she said. "The men make allowances for each other. They won't tell you about the men they don't want to work with."[6]

Women were just as effective as men, she stated, "and in some instances better, because they might prevent violence from happening."[7] This was a well-known truth since the early days of women in policing and was something Mae knew from her first days on the force. She thought the issue was more about fear of women taking men's jobs or the wives worried about their husbands alone in a patrol car with a female cop. Why punish the women if wives couldn't trust their husbands?

Even in the 1940s, when Gertie and her compatriots were joining the NYPD, women were held to higher standards than men and were required to hold college degrees. Male applicants were not. Mae later commented on the educational requirements, saying simply that policewomen "must have the technique to know what to do in any situation."[8]

Of course, Mae's education in police work, investigating, counseling, testifying, and understanding the consequences for society as the result of crime— all of it beyond those early classes in the basics—had all come through a master's-level course called tough firsthand experience. By 1941, she thought she'd seen and done it all.

One afternoon, she left work a bit early and took herself out for a treat. It was an unusually warm and humid March day in New York, and Mae thought she might just take in a movie, sit in the dark in an air-conditioned theater swirling with the artificial breezes, and relax. So she bought her ticket for the matinee, and through force of habit, she scanned the rows of other moviegoers for anyone with ill intentions. She didn't see any potential seat tippers, pickpockets, or murderers. All clear, she settled in with her bag of popcorn and cream soda and prepared to turn off her overactive investigative brain and simply enjoy herself.

Mae was excited about the main feature. She looked forward to this one, the new movie with Barbara Stanwyck and Henry Fonda—*The Lady Eve*. They were among her favorite movie stars, but the big attraction for Mae was the setting and plot for the movie. The storyline was about a con artist (Barbara Stanwyck) who along with her two cronies were card sharks, fleecing the other passengers on an ocean cruise. Eve was a sharp card player and a lousy flirt. Mae had nearly finished her popcorn by the time Eve fell in love with Henry Fonda's character, a naive young man, the heir to a brewery and its fortune.

The sweet bubble of the movie's happy ending burst as Mae left the theater and blinked in the harsh afternoon sunlight and the blasting cacophony of taxi horns. Mae sighed and trudged off to her little cottage in Jackson Heights, but she longed for something more. A good, long ocean cruise where she could lose herself in the fantasy life of the rich and famous. Not that she planned to fall for any con artist or card shark.

On Sunday morning, March 23, Mae sat at her dining room table with the plump *New York Times* and the somewhat smaller Sunday edition of the

Brooklyn Daily Eagle. The *Eagle's* front-page story let her know in no uncertain terms that she wouldn't be heading out on a cruise to Europe any time soon. The headline blared, "Nazi Fleet Sweeps Atlantic for New Victims After Reich Claims Record Toll of 33 Ships."

Mae turned the page, sipped her coffee, and kept on scanning. She usually read every single article in the Sunday paper, but not today. When the news was bad, as most of it was in those days, she just skipped ahead. Then an advertisement caught her eye. Right there on page 46.

It was a full quarter page, announcing that the Great White Fleet was promoting its cruises to Central America. "Give life the lift it needs!" the ad proclaimed. "Cruise gaily out to venturesome days…to the magic of colorful ports and sunny hours bright with fun."[9]

Before the war, Mae would never even have considered a visit to Central America. Sure, she'd cruised through the Panama Canal but not into any of the other countries in the region. This itinerary certainly looked promising though. She put her cold coffee aside and kept reading. The sixteen-day cruise left New York on Fridays and included the Panama Canal Zone, Costa Rica, Guatemala, and Havana, Cuba. Every other cruise substituted Nassau, Bahamas, or Kingston, Jamaica, for Havana.

It wasn't the classic European cruise she'd grown to love, but it definitely had some potential. That promise included onboard "outdoor pools, spacious sports decks, splendid orchestras, famed service,"[10] and all the staterooms were designated as first class. Mae was sold.

She sailed to Central America in June, earlier than her usual vacation time, but then she didn't want to be sweating in the jungles of Guatemala when temperatures were at the height of summer. She timed it too so that she could visit Jamaica, having already seen Havana and Honduras in 1932. Maybe she'd stay onboard during one of the port days and lounge by the pool instead. It wouldn't be crowded, and she could indulge in a new beverage, perhaps a piña colada. Mae was always up for something new.

Ancon transiting the Panama Canal in 1939. (Source: Wikimedia Commons.)

It was a lovely cruise, she thought later, but not quite as elegant as her European excursions. The ship, the *Ancon*, wasn't truly the same European-style first class that Mae was used to, but for sixteen days, Mae was able to relax in the sun and enjoy the tropical warmth. Besides, the ship actually featured real coffee. No rationing there.

The *Ancon* sailed its last season as a cruise liner in 1941. By 1942, she was taken over by the Army Transport Service and used for troop transport to Europe. The *Ancon* served as the flagship coordinating operations in support of American forces landing on Omaha Beach on D-Day in 1944. By August 1945, she was parked in Tokyo Bay to witness the Japanese surrender.

But Mae knew none of that. She only knew that options for travel escape were becoming more and more limited and the majority of her plans would be placed on hold for the duration of the war. In fact, war in Europe and the Pacific was coming home to New York in ways that Mae thought had ended with the dissolution of the Bund. She was still working on cases of potential sabotage and wondering daily what the world was coming to.

December 7, 1941, dawned as a bright, sharply sunny day in New York City, a bit chilly and breezy, but it looked like a nice afternoon for a walk through the neighborhood. Mae had the radio on in her kitchen as she gathered up the Sunday papers, having spent the morning perusing them from front to back. Then she stopped in her tracks at the special announcement on the radio. All servicemen and women were being ordered to return to their stations.

Something was wrong, Mae knew. She looked at the phone. Something major was happening. Would the police also be recalled? They were in charge of coordinating civil defense of the city after all. But that day, despite her waiting and watching, the call didn't come. By suppertime the news bulletins were coming in to announce that Pearl Harbor had been bombed. As dusk approached, the announcements changed, telling New Yorkers to take precautions and "Cover all windows and do not allow any light to escape. Do not use the telephone because all telephone lines at this time must be reserved for the government."[11]

Just then, the telephone shrilled. Mae jumped, but she knew already it wasn't the 108th calling. It had to be the girls.

"Mom, have you heard the news? What are we going to do? What if they draft Fred? I don't want him to go in the army. I won't know what to do without him!" Florence sounded frantic.

"You need to stay off the phone, hon. Why don't you come over tomorrow for supper and we can talk about it. Okay?"

"But, Mom, what if Fred is drafted right away?" Florence started to cry.

"Now, now. I'm sure that Fred won't be called up tomorrow. But right now, honey, I need to keep the line open so the station can reach me if I'm needed. Don't worry. It is all going to be fine. We'll talk soon. Bye-bye now. Love you." Mae hung up.

A second later, the phone rang again.

Of course, the other one had to check in too. "Mom! What do you think? Is the department calling back all the cops? What's going to happen here? Do you have the scoop?"

"Grace, honey, I have to keep the line open if my boss calls. I promise I'll tell you everything just as soon as I know. You can come over tomorrow with your sister, and we can all have a nice visit. Love you. Good night."

Mae put the phone firmly back into its cradle and stared at it as though daring it to ring again. It didn't. She turned out the lights and pulled back the curtains, staring out into the street. Everything was dark, as far as she could see. Not even a glow on the horizon from the big city lights in Manhattan.

Mae knew she wouldn't sleep at all that night or for many to come. Would the station call? She didn't know. She was still processing the weight of what was happening, how everything was different now.

America was at war.

CHAPTER 14
DÉJÀ VU

Wartime culture settled onto New York like a worn blanket with those scratchy old habits of caution and fear, and Mae felt that sense of past wartime customs and manners repeating themselves. The challenges of young women flocking to the city to chase young men startled some, but Mae had seen that before. Women moving into men's jobs when they would have been criticized for doing so just a few years earlier was also familiar, as were the still sharp fears of Nazi sympathizers hiding in plain sight, plus the threats of communists and mobsters expanding their operations into wartime profiteering.

New York sent 850,000 men to military service in World War II, more than any other city in the United States. With women moving into the workforce, sometimes the city seemed unnaturally quiet during the day. Wartime deprivation was keenly felt, although much of it was due to rationing rather than scarcity. Horsemeat was shipped in from the Midwest, since beef was gone from the stores. Many couldn't even afford horsemeat, and the mayor had to forbid begging in the subways. Orphanages were filling up as families couldn't care for their children, and cases of juvenile delinquency were on the rise.[1]

Late one afternoon in the 108th Precinct break room, Mae read a news-paper article about the so-called new wave of women entering the ranks of the NYPD. Reporter Mary Elizabeth Plummer described the average policewoman thus: "She may be fresh from college and wear a bow on her pageboy bob...or she may be a young matron, a widow, or a white-haired woman in her fifties."[2]

Mae harumphed. After all, her hair was still brown. Well, there may have been a few strands of gray, but not many. And those that did dare appear fell victim to her tweezers.

"She's likely to be slim but strong and muscular, rather than Amazonian," the article continued.[3] Mae grumbled again. Could that reporter be referring to her long-ago title as the Amazon of New York?

"She'd better not be thinking about me," Mae said aloud. The reporter wasn't, it seemed. Mae wasn't mentioned. She lost interest in the rest of the article, tossing the paper aside.

Even as men were signing up for military service and women were head-ing to factories and other parts of the workforce, the department's roster was shrinking. More women did apply to join the force, college graduates all, spurred on by the relentless messaging of popular icons like Rosie the Riveter. Rosie, with her red-and-white polka-dot bandanna, flexed her biceps and urged women on with her "We can do it!" motto.[4]

And every woman was an asset as crime was on the rise. New York never declined in criminal activity. It only repeated itself in cycles and continued to grow and expand in new and inventive ways. Mae thought she could write a book about it. The cycles were predictable even if the creativity of the crimi-nal mind was always able to surprise and shock. Plus, wartime missions were piling on. The police were involved in coordinating air raid procedures, drills, and protection, training the City Patrol Corps (CPC) and assuming other civic support actions.

In December 1941, Fort Totten had been designated as the headquarters of the antiaircraft unit of the Eastern Defense Command. It wasn't far from Mae's home, located strategically at Willets Point peninsula on Long Island's north shore.[5] The command was responsible for the defense of New York City and Long Island. In fact, that site had been designated as New York City's first line of defense since the Revolutionary War. There was an antiaircraft battery at Greenwood Cemetery in Brooklyn, plus another that Mae knew of in Rockaway Park in Queens. That was comforting, Mae thought. Plus she was absolutely certain her neighbors would rise up should the enemy, those Nazis and their American fans, even consider launching an attack on U.S. soil. She had her .38 service revolver cleaned and at the ready too.

While the big guns charged with the mission of defending New York were part of several different command organizations during the war, all citizens had to contend with the requirements to prepare themselves for the worst. Buy bonds. Start a garden. Save scrap. Use ration books as required. And keep those lights *off*.

Practice blackouts started just a week after the Japanese attack on Pearl Harbor. The new version, "dimouts," didn't take effect until May 1942. Dimouts meant that there was a bit of outdoor lighting, but it was faint. All lights, including those on theater marquees, had to point downward. This was especially disconcerting to playgoers accustomed to the bright lights of Broadway and in Times Square. Mae missed those clever, flashy signs, a million bulbs boldly lighting up the night sky with all their exuberance and pride. They symbolized American freedom to her and to hundreds of thousands of others as well. She yearned to see the "Peanuts that endlessly tumbled from a Planters bag" on one massive bright sign, missed "the swimming fish in the Wrigley billboard of lights." Further down Broadway, it just didn't seem right that the orange Sunkist sunburst was all frozen and dark.[6] No more massive spinning fruit silhouetted against the night sky. And while the unlit Camel cigarettes sign stood quietly, its gray smoke rings still billowed out over the darkened street, puffing from an invisible source. Even at home, all lights had to point down and be invisible from the street. But the darkest days were yet to come.

In February 1942, a French ship was docked in New York Harbor, being refitted for service with the U.S. Navy. A luxury ocean liner built in France in 1931, the SS *Normandie* was acquired by the U.S. Navy just weeks after Pearl Harbor, on December 27, 1941. She had just been redesignated as the USS *Lafayette* when she mysteriously caught fire and capsized. Luckily no one was on board at the time. The ship lay on her side for much of the next year, looking not only like hope abandoned but displaying a warning of what was to come. Eventually she was towed to the Brooklyn Navy Yard and was sold for scrap following the war.[7]

Coming just two months after the attack at Pearl Harbor, everyone immediately assumed the incident was the result of enemy sabotage. The navy's investigators visited District Attorney Thomas Dewey and asked to meet with Mafia leaders to see what they could learn from their networks about suspect dockworkers and infiltrators. Eventually they made their way to Clinton Prison in Dannemora, New York. Hundreds of miles from New York, the dark prison known as "Siberia" had been home to Lucky Luciano for six years since his conviction for pandering. He was quickly moved to a site more accessible to investigators, Great Meadow, in Comstock.[8] This was more of a country club–type prison. While Luciano talked eagerly with investigators, he also met with a number of his old friends and business associates. He desperately wanted out of prison and was willing to find any way possible to make that happen. It was alleged that he had approved, through his network, the sabotage of the *Lafayette*. Naval intelligence personnel weren't aware of this rumor when they suggested to Luciano that his support in preventing future acts of sabotage might lead to his release. He agreed, and supposedly his family of informants and spies kept the docks and troop ships safe for the remainder of the war.

But according to later research, the ship's fire and capsizing was nothing more than an unlucky accident. A spark from a welder's torch had apparently ignited a pile of nearby life jackets, and the fire spread. But public suspicions continued and rumors ran rampant. Spreading hysteria over the incident led to the launching of a number of investigations, by the navy, FBI, U.S. Senate, House of Representatives, New York City Fire Department, and Manhattan district attorney's office. In the end, all ruled out sabotage.[9]

But the rumors continued and worked to Lucky Luciano's advantage. Investigators continued to visit him, and he kept talking. Luciano also wanted to help out his favorite U.S. Army general, George C. Patton. He provided information to the FBI to pass on—just some insights and local intelligence that the general might find useful in his campaign planning in Europe. There were also rumors that Luciano had paid moneys into Dewey's gubernatorial campaign. While the web of innuendo, suppositions, and lies were entangled beyond the ability of investigators to see the reality of some of these actions, the results were clear. On January 3, 1945, then Governor Thomas Dewey commuted Luciano's sentence. Three days later, he was deported.[10]

Just after midnight on June 13, 1942, four men landed on Long Island in a rubber boat. They were delivered by a German U-boat that pulled up on a sandbar to release them for a two-year mission of sabotage and destruction. Let by German agent John Dasch, the spies unloaded weapons and explosives onto the beach and then began to bury their Nazi uniforms in the sand. Another group of four were sent to Florida, landing on Ponte Vedra Beach. The New York group was unlucky, being stopped almost immediately by a

Coast Guard officer out walking patrol. Ensign John Cullen questioned the so-called sailors briefly, then accepted a bribe of $300 to not disclose what he'd seen. He then turned and reported them immediately.[11]

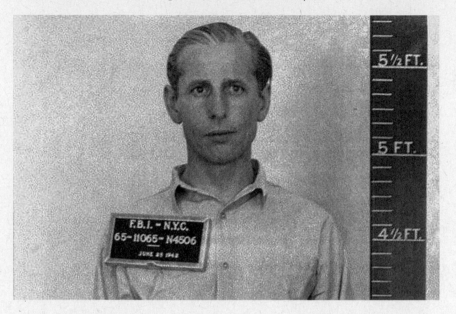

George John Dasch, German Agent. (FBI photo, New York City, June 25, 1942.)

The saboteurs intended to blow up bridges, factories, and trains, supporting Hitler's war effort by wreaking havoc across America and destroying as much of her industrial base and supply lines as possible. But just days later, all eight spies were in custody and tried by a military commission in Washington. One received a sentence of thirty years, another a life sentence, and the other six executed.[12]

Mae worked that case with the FBI and investigated hundreds of other reports of attempted Nazi sabotage and mysterious infiltrators. She followed up on every tip, every call, and every related complaint. She even sought out some of the witnesses from Lucky Luciano's trial and asked them what they knew. But no other acts of sabotage or incursions onto American soil were found during the war. There were plenty of reports of sabotage though and numbers of aliens attempting access to the U.S., often posing as American citizens. One arrested in New York was a German, Karl Horst, posing as an American soldier with amnesia. According to the FBI, there were 16,000 aliens and posers arrested and over 20,000 claims of sabotage investigated.[13]

Investigations were tedious and often painstaking work, but Mae never skipped a step, avoided a call, or failed to follow up on a possible connection. She knew it was due to their vigilance—of all law enforcement agencies and the military, guarding the coastal approaches and the skies. It was intense, serious work, and she couldn't talk about it. The story of spies on Long Island wasn't widely known until 2011 when the British released recently declassified documents.[14]

By July 1943, Mae's son-in-law Fred Evans and his brother had enlisted in the army, and Florence was at loose ends. She came over one Sunday afternoon just a few months after Fred left for training to talk to Mae about her plans. Mae was busy ironing her uniform while Florence sipped her cup of real coffee, heavily laced with cream and a small mountain of sugar. Mae smiled at Florence's obvious enjoyment. She needed a little bit of a treat. So what if Mae had very little sugar left in her ration allotment?

She followed Florence's gaze over to the kitchen counter. A box of Kraft macaroni and cheese sat there, waiting to be cooked for dinner. Mae smiled to herself, waited for the question.

"You making that for supper, Mom?" Florence asked. "Where did you get it? I haven't seen any in stores for a long time."

"Oh, I've been saving it for a special occasion." Mae couldn't look at her, or she knew she'd laugh.

"Mom! You got that from my kitchen, didn't you?"

"Why, Florence! How could you say such a thing?" One hand on her heart, Mae tried for an innocent look and failed. She set down the iron.

"Look at the back of the box, Mom. You see that little tick mark right there by the word 'cheese'?"

"Yes. There it is. So?"

"So I put that there before you came to visit me last week. Just a test, Mother dear. Just a test."

"You got me this time, Florence," Mae admitted. "Caught red-handed. You'd make a great undercover detective." They both had a good laugh over their back-and-forth kitchen thievery. "So now let's just share it," Mae declared. She picked up the iron again.

"Good idea, Mom." Florence grinned. "Later we can talk about that can of Spam you have hidden."

"Okay, dear. But let's talk about Fred for a moment first." Mae cleared her throat. "Why don't you stay with me while he's away in the Pacific? Or whatever secret place they're sending him to," Mae said, flipping over a navy-blue sleeve. She peered at Florence through a cloud of steam.

"I don't know, Mom. I know how you like your independence. I'm just afraid I'm going to get pretty lonely with Fred gone. Not to mention hungry."

"And you're going to worry yourself to death if you don't have something to keep you busy. You know you're truly welcome to move back in with me."

"That sounds perfect. Plus, you work so hard, Mom. All those long hours. I'm glad to help out. But I have another idea."

"All right," Mae said with a smile. "I don't think we'll get in each other's way, and given the way this war is going, it could be a long while before Fred gets leave to come home. You can make the basement into your own little apartment and save your rent money. You'll have a nice little nest egg built up by the time he returns," Mae added.

"Thanks, Mom. You know the army sends me a little money from his check, but the mail is so slow. I haven't heard from Fred in weeks. But this will work for all of us. I'll start packing up. Not that there's all that much to pack. By the way, how's Grace doing? I haven't seen baby Bobby in weeks now."

Mae sighed inwardly. Florence may have thought she was being subtle; she was anything but. She wished the girls would just talk with each other instead of relying on her to relay messages back and forth. "Little Robert is doing just fine. I'm sure she'll bring him over to visit soon." Mae tried to will the subject closed. It didn't work.

"And what's going on with her and Ted? Do you think they'll get back together soon?"

"Now, Florence…"

"No, really, Mother. They've been separated for what, three years now? Four? That's just not normal. Maybe I'll just ask her whenever I see her." Florence stuck out her chin. She wanted answers.

"I do want you two to talk. But she may not be ready to discuss her marriage. If, and only if, she wants to talk about her relationship with Ted, she will. And my advice to you is don't push. Your sister has been through enough with that man and his temper. She doesn't need to think about him at all." Mae gave her daughter the policewoman look, the one her girls called the "you're under arrest" stare. It always got results—confessions, agreements, or even silence. Whatever she wanted.

"Oh, Mother. Fine, I promise I won't say a word about Ted. But I do worry about her. Sometimes she seems so sad. And it's pretty obvious he's done her wrong, one way or another. I just wish I could help her somehow."

"You do help. You babysit Bobby so she can have a break once in a while. And you're a good listener. We just need to be supportive right now. That's all." The less Florence knew about Ted's alleged battering, the better. A few months earlier, Mae had several of her detective friends visit Grace's husband, Ted. They persuaded him that it would be in his best interest to move out.

Neither daughter knew Mae's role in Ted's departure. Mae thought it better that way. But at least he was out of Grace's life.

"I can do that, Mom. I'm very supportive."

"I know you are, sweetie." Mae patted Florence's hand. "Now, what was this idea you had?"

Florence unfolded the *Long Island Daily Press* to a full-page advertisement, grandly seeking to recruit new members for the City Patrol Corps (CPC).

"The CPC, Flo?" Mae frowned. Then she composed herself and attempted to look interested, if not approving.

The CPC reminded Mae of her time with the Women's Police Reserve. She hadn't thought of either of her girls doing anything like this. Florence would be good at it though. She could handle just about anything. When the girls were little, she always watched out for Grace. She'd comfort her when she fell off the swing, check out Grace's friends in school, and defend her when she'd forgotten to make her bed. She would be good at looking out for neighbors in any kind of a watch program.

"What would you be doing, dear?"

"Mom, that's the best part. I'd be right here in Queens. This ad is for the Queens branch of the CPC. So I wouldn't have to go anywhere. And I'd be making a little money of my own."

Mae hummed, pressing steam into the pockets of her uniform jacket. She liked the idea. Florence would be busy and making a contribution to the war effort. It might help her from worrying about Fred, and she could also be closer to Grace and Mae. It would be good to have both girls close, Mae thought.

Florence looked down at the paper, eagerly running her finger over the page. Mae looked down at the top of Florence's head, so serious about this new opportunity. Mae was glad Florence had found this as a goal. She looked excited, and Mae realized she could really make something of the new opportunity this represented.

"Mom, are you listening?"

"Mm-hmm. Remind me what the duties are again?" Mae had learned this technique while watching sparring attorneys during many a boring jury trial. They just asked to have the main points of the argument emphasized again and again, hoping that jurors were still awake and listening. And Mae wanted Florence to express her goals again, clarifying them for herself.

"It says the women's unit furnishes transportation and provides clerical and administrative services for the CPC. The men have to patrol in the evenings in four-hour shifts, either from four to eight or eight to midnight. This is much better than all that stomping around the men do. And it's better than giving blood, buying war bonds, or being an air warden. I wonder if they have coffee in their offices." Florence looked down at her empty cup.

"I don't know. Where is their headquarters, Flo?"

"Um, it says Richmond Hill. That's not too far from here."

"Less than ten miles," Mae agreed, although it was closer to where Florence was living now in Ozone Park. "Might take you a bit to get there depending on traffic."

Florence nodded. Mae wondered if her daughter was planning to borrow her car. Fred had sold theirs when he left.

"Well, there is a form to fill out. Why don't you put your name in and see what they say. Here, I've got an envelope. You get it ready, and I'll drop it in the mail tomorrow."

Mae mailed the application the next day, and Florence was interviewed and accepted for the CPC weeks later. She worked part-time and moved in with Mae, busying herself tending to the flowers in the front bed and the victory garden in the back and writing daily letters to Fred. Mae was glad to see her busy and involved. Now if she could just figure out what to do about Grace.

One day, Mae put one of the extra kitchen chairs out on the narrow front stoop and sat down. The battered chair creaked as she settled in, letting the day wash away while she contemplated the war, her daughters, and life in general. It was a meditation to have that quiet moment. Soon she was out there most evenings when she came home from work. She watched the commuters straggle home, the kids playing in the street, the gradual slowing of traffic and people beginning to move indoors for the evening. The Homeowners Association wouldn't permit the residents to build porches on the front of their cottages, but Mae had her place on the stoop.

On August 19, 1944, Mae's second grandson, John William, arrived. Florence still had a million prying questions for her younger sister, but Mae managed to stave them off. A few weeks later, on one mild Sunday afternoon, she grabbed a second kitchen chair and pulled Grace out onto the stoop beside her. Florence stayed inside with the sleeping baby and Bobby, playing with his Tinkertoys on the floor.

"How are you doing, Grace?" Mae asked.

"I'm fine, Mom. I'm so glad you got to meet Mr. John Carr at the hospital. He's been just wonderful, and I know the more you get to know him, the more you'll like him. Ted is sending me money and staying away, which is just fine with me. Sometimes I think you must have had something to do with him leaving. I never thought he would actually go quietly. Or go without hurting me again."

"Hmm." Mae nodded, noncommittal. She looked down at Grace's arm, the scars from cigarette burns still visible. Grace noticed, tugged at the sleeve of her sweater.

"I know you don't want to say anything about what you did, Mom, but thank you anyway. And Florence. I know she's really curious about what's going on with me but I just can't talk about it yet."

"I understand. One day, when you're ready, you two can work it out."

"We will. And after the war, we'll all be one big family again. Florence and Fred, me and John. And the boys."

"I look forward to that," Mae said. Normal times.

"As soon as his kids are grown and out of the house, John is going to divorce his wife and we can get married. That might take a couple of years but it will all work out."

"I understand. You don't have any problems with gossipy neighbors?" Mae asked.

"No, not since I moved again. There is enough trouble in the world today. No one is interested in me or the boys or where my husband is. Just Florence."

"She loves you, you know." Mae put her hand over Grace's.

"I know, Mom. I love her too. And she just dotes on Bobby. I think he's going to stay her favorite."

"It looks that way. But right now, I hear the baby fussing."

"I'll go see," Grace said. She paused at the front door. "I love you, Mom."

"Love you too, Gracie," Mae replied.

She leaned back and closed her eyes, letting the September sun warm her face. Mae felt that maybe now she could afford the time to take a trip. Her family was growing, and one day soon, it would be complete, when they could all be together. In the meantime, there was still that old familiar itch. Where to go that wasn't only safe from the war zones but actually possible? Most cruise ships had been requisitioned by the military, so that was out of the question. Maybe she'd escape the winter this year, go south to Florida.

Florence had been there before with Judge James Foley and friends, visiting Florida's east coast with some of her father's family members from his first marriage. Of course, that trip occurred years ago, just after John passed away in January 1928. She regaled Mae regularly with her stories of how wonderful it was to lounge about at the luxurious Royal Poinciana Hotel in Palm Beach. They had cocktails on the veranda every afternoon and dressed for dinner. She had a scrapbook from her Florida visit, and one article she'd underlined noted, "The Brooklyn Colony always takes part in Washington's Birthday celebrations."[15]

But that wasn't quite what Mae was looking for. She didn't want to be part of a group traveling together from New York. She wanted to be away from it all, from being part of a pack of tourists. Maybe St. Petersburg, Florida, she thought. Mae picked a hotel from several brochures she found in a library. The Surf Club sounded like fun, like the beaches she'd visited in Central America. Sunny, warm, and lots of fun, with a steel drum band and a tiki bar and a sweet drink in a coconut with an umbrella to top it off.

It seemed the war was going in the right direction by the holidays. Florence received a holiday package from Fred, stationed somewhere in the Philippines. Inside there was a pearl necklace for Florence and two heavy, silver-plated little mugs for their nephews to have their milk in for breakfast. The mugs were engraved with Bobby's and Johnny's names and birthdates. They loved them. Mae thought things were going as well as they could be. The girls were on friendly terms—the holiday gifts had certainly helped with that—and she felt like she could leave for a bit without worrying.

In January 1945, she packed her car and gave Florence a list of places she planned to stop and stay and the phone numbers of the hotels. Away she went, her grand departure suddenly slowed as she drove straight into a snow squall. But that didn't slow Mae, not one bit. She drove straight through, not stopping until she reached the Sunshine State and her goal: twenty glorious days of sparkling sand and long afternoons just listening to the ocean's rhythm.

The bands and raucous nightlife, well, she enjoyed all that too. Mostly as an observer but it was wonderful seeing people begin to enjoy themselves again, despite the war and world just outside Florida's sunny bubble.

CHAPTER 15

SNOWBIRD

May 7, 1945, Victory in Europe Day, meant the beginning of explosive victory celebrations across the five boroughs of New York City. That day, Times Square and Wall Street came roaring back to life with a no-holds-barred, raucous street party that rocked the city. People thronged the streets cheering while the voice of Mayor La Guardia blared from a loudspeaker, telling people to behave themselves. Ticker tape rained down on the crowds, and newspapers sailed through the air. World War I veterans waved small American flags, kids wondered if they'd get a day off from school, while young girls kissed soldiers with overseas bars, whispering suggestively, "You'll never go back now."[1]

The Statue of Liberty awakened, her torch blazing. The lights of Broadway began to sing. Mothers everywhere rejoiced in their premature Mother's Day gift from the European front. Those with sons in the Pacific still prayed. But Mae was happy, as was everyone else. Everywhere she went, people were celebrating life and freedom.

The celebrations continued for months on end. There were any number of ticker-tape parades, and the streets of Manhattan stayed drenched in a rainbow of happy litter. Mae, her daughters, and her grandsons were crowding the sidewalks on June 20 for the victory parade celebrating the hero, General Dwight D. Eisenhower, the supreme allied commander. Bobby waved a tiny American flag at the white-haired World War I veterans along the parade route; they all waved back. Slumped in his carriage, ten-month-old Johnny slept through the uproar. The family cheered along with four million other New Yorkers as Ike waved at the crowds and confetti fell all around them like candy-colored snow.[2] It was history in the making and Mae didn't want to miss a moment of it.

As soon as President Harry Truman announced the Japanese surrender on August 14, celebrations erupted in Times Square once again. Sailors pushed each other up lampposts to unfurl American flags, and ticker tape swirled through the air, drifting down again on the throngs below.[3]

Even as she could hear the cheers all the way from Manhattan, Mae found that this time she was more relieved than cheerful. It was finally over and she was *glad*. Meanwhile, Florence was ecstatic. Now she *knew* her husband Fred would soon be making his way home. Mae was ready for a quiet return to normal, whatever the new normal might turn out to be.

All around, it seemed like the end of an era. District Attorney Thomas Dewey had left the city behind in 1942 and was well established in the governor's mansion in Albany. There were rumors he would run for president next. Mayor La Guardia announced his retirement, scheduling it for the end of the year, and Police Commissioner Lewis Valentine was also on the way out. The two had steered the city from the worst of the Depression through the strains of the war years. Valentine had survived in the job as commissioner for eleven years, longer than any other commissioner up to that point. La Guardia recognized his accomplishments, noting the job of police commissioner was "the toughest in the city."[4] But their time was done.

It was as though the departures of the city leaders were whispering in Mae's ear on the way out the door. "It's time to go. Start something new. Fly away."

She brushed off the thoughts as she always did with something she wasn't ready to think about. Not yet. There were still things to do at work, things to do at home. Important things. Mae never lost track of what led her to a life in law enforcement in the first place: that desire to help, to protect and make a difference in the lives of women and children in the city. She couldn't just up and quit on protecting the vulnerable, could she? Leave them to fend for themselves at the hands of criminals? No, she couldn't.

These thoughts were tumbling around in her head like old shoes in an electric dryer. They were just slapping back and forth, from memory to unfulfilled need and back again, not helping her one bit to focus on the future in a rational way.

One Friday morning, she took the subway over to the 103rd Precinct, hoping to catch up with a few of her friends there and set up a bunco game night. But when she walked into the station, the desk sergeant spotted her right away.

"Hey, Mae, what you doing here? This isn't your house." Mikey Panzarella stood up, yawning, his girth rising and falling like a mighty mountain.

"I know, Mikey. I'm just visiting. Is Eloise around?"

"Nah, she had a doctor appointment, she said. Some women's thing." He flipped his hand back and forth, noncommittal. No details.

"Don't ask, Mikey. Trust me, you don't want to know."

"Don't worry, I won't. But hey, since you're here, you mind giving a lady prisoner a once-over? Couple patrolmen just brought her a couple minutes ago. Said she was D and D."

"My, my. Drunk and disorderly in your upscale neighborhood. And it isn't even noon yet. Imagine that."

"I know! Guys think she was soliciting too. Got to pay for that habit somehow. She's been charged."

"Drugs or just booze?" It made a difference in their behavior, Mae knew. She didn't want to face any belligerent drunk, or an aggressive drug addict for that matter.

"Dunno, Mae. You tell me. She reeks."

Mae sighed and looked down at her nice dress and heels. Sure, she'd do a good turn for the 103rd. "Okay, Mikey. I'll go on back." Mae held out her hand for the keys to the holding cell. She put her purse with her .38 police revolver into one of the small weapons lockers in the break room and snapped it shut, turning the lock.

This purse was a new version of the one she'd been issued over ten years earlier. Now a shoulder bag, it had room not only for her service weapon but also for makeup and lipstick. Mae never forgot the advice from then mayor Fiorello La Guardia: "Use your gun as you would your lipstick. Use it only when you need it and use it intelligently. Don't overdo either one."[5]

Then she traipsed down the dark hallway and gazed into a darkened, shadowy holding cell. There was a woman lying on her side facing the wall, her back to the door. Mae could hear her sniffling.

"Mrs. Osborne, I'm Detective Foley, here to examine you. Would you mind getting up, please?" Mae flipped the lights on, stepped inside, locked the cell door, and pocketed the key.

"Get out," the woman slurred. "I'm havin' a nap here."

"I'm afraid I can't do that just yet. I need to check you now for any weapons or possible injuries. Please get up and stand here with your arms outstretched. I'm going to pat you down. It will only take a moment."

The sniffling stopped. There was a long pause. Mae held her breath. What was it going to be? Compliance or…

"You bitch!" The woman flew off the cot with an unholy shriek and cracked Mae across the face with an open hand. Mae was knocked backward, her head hitting the bars. Stunned, she shook herself and put up an arm, but the woman reared back and headbutted her right in the solar plexus.

"Guard!" Mae called out, but she was already on the floor coughing, and the woman was kicking her in the stomach, the back, the head. "Guard!"

Two hulking patrolmen rushed in and slammed the prizefighting Mrs. Osborne onto the floor, but not before she landed a roundhouse punch on one of them, breaking his nose. They cuffed her hands behind her back and held her in place.

"Holy Mother of God, Mae, are you okay?" The other officer asked, taking out his handkerchief. He pointed at Mae's eyebrow. She wiped blood off her forehead as he helped her up. She wobbled a moment, felt her hands shake as she looked down at the bloody handkerchief.

"I'm fine, boys. But I'm getting too old for these fisticuffs, I tell you." She tried a weak laugh, but her ribs hurt. The patrolmen tried to smile with her. "All right then. Keep your hands on her shoulders, boys. Mrs. Osborne, you're still getting searched. And, gentlemen, let's make certain that she is charged with assault on a police officer."

"Gladly," they said in unison, holding the prisoner tightly while Mae did her job.

Afterward, she limped up to the front desk. "Thanks a lot, Mikey. You owe me one." She took a glance in the mirror behind the desk. One eye was starting to close. "Jesus, Mary, and Joseph. I look a sight," she exclaimed.

"Aw, I'm really sorry this one was such a loser, Mae. You need to go see a doctor." Mikey looked like he was going to vomit. This was all his fault.

"What I need is an ice pack and some aspirin. Will you call the 108th for me? Let them know I'm taking a sick day. Maybe two."

He agreed but insisted that a patrol car take Mae home. She wasn't riding the subway after that. No, sir.

Once home, Mae gingerly washed up and changed into her nightgown. Florence got out two ice packs and, with an exaggerated sigh at the labor required, refilled the ice cube trays for later. Lying in bed, Mae had ample time to think hard about cracking open that doorway to retirement. She was fifty-seven, an age when most officers were more than ready to turn in the shield. She had the years of service too, twenty-two, going back to her appointment in 1923. Her pension was guaranteed by New York City's Police Life and Health Insurance Fund, under the first municipal disability fund. The fund's investment system was revised in 1940, but Mae was grandfathered by the old system.[6]

She had financial security. That wasn't an issue. And if the day's events had taught her anything, it was that it was definitely time to toss her tin into a bureau drawer and head for the door herself. Maybe. She drifted off to sleep, putting the big question aside.

By the time Mae was considering retirement from the force, only three women had made it up the steep ladder to the rank of detective first grade. The first was Mae's role model from before she joined the force, Isabella Goodwin. Isabella's exploits were legendary in the NYPD. She was most well known for her work with the Vice Squad and breaking open the case of a series of taxicab thefts. Mary Shanley was the second to reach that rank, and Mary Sullivan was the third. Director of the Women's Police Bureau since 1926, Mary Sullivan retired not long after Mae Foley turned in her shield. Mary Sullivan served for thirty years and was sixty-five when she decided it was time. Like Mae, Mary planned to travel in her retirement.[7]

The thought of new adventures spurred Mae to her final decision. By the end of the week, her mind was made up. In early December, she submitted her retirement paperwork, and in her heart, she knew she was ready to make the change. When asked about her decision, she said simply that she wanted time to travel again. "I had to get leaves of absence to travel before," she explained. "Always I had to be back to a certain place by a certain time. Now I can go ahead and do it on my own. Go where I please, and most important, stay as long as I please."[8]

Of course, overseas travel would still have to wait. Postwar Europe wasn't ready for tourists. That would take years. And so many cruise ships had been requisitioned for wartime service that they required extensive dry dock renovations and refitting for commercial passenger service. But that didn't mean Mae had to wait to start her next chapter.

She had a plan. Because Mae always had a plan. She was going to split her time, north and south. Fly away to Florida just as soon as she could and stay put in the Sunshine State until the daffodils bloomed by her front stoop back in Queens. Only then would she return. She just wished she could take her grandsons with her. They would have such a good time on the beach, building sandcastles and chasing the tides while they looked for shells. She could teach them to swim. But Grace didn't look as though she was ready to let them run off with their grandma. Not just yet anyway. Maybe when they were a little bit older.

As the announcement of her retirement became public, Mae found herself the subject of a number of feature stories by eager New York City newspaper reporters. At last she felt a bit more comfortable talking to the press than she had in the early days, although she downplayed the most dangerous exploits of her career and was always a bit grudging with the details of her work. Some things she never did reveal. "Pistol Packing Mama" they called her admiringly. And "Long Island's Famous Policewoman." Not the "Amazon of New York."

Mae took it all in stride, but once her mind was made up, she was ready to go *now*. The *Long Island Star Journal* exclaimed excitedly, "She's not even waiting to take the twenty-three day leave to which she's entitled in January. She leaves for Florida on New Year's Day."[9]

THEY CAME HERE

Famous Policewoman From New York Held Her Own With Tough Characters

By GEORGE BARTLETT

New York's most famous policewoman has come to St. Petersburg to live.

She is Mae V. Foley, for 30 years a member of the New York Police Department, organizer and president of Manhattan's Women's Police Reserves and now the only honorary woman member of the Retired Police Association of North America, which has its headquarters here.

To meet Mrs. Foley you would probably not suspect her calling. Mild mannered and affable, her brawn is concealed behind a well-groomed exterior. Yet in her day Mae Foley scuffled with many of New York's toughest characters, and never came out second best.

Born in the famous "gas house district" of the lower East Side, of Irish and French ancestry, she grew up in a rugged environment where few but the hardy survive. Her family was politically minded and it was through her brother, chief clerk in the New York Supreme Court's appelate division, that she secured a job as clerk in the City Tenement House Department when she was 17. Later she served as case worker in the welfare department and as probate clerk in Surrogate's Court.

In 1915, with war looming and policemen going into the Army, she was called upon by Police Inspector James Dwyer to organize 7,000 women into the Women's Police Reserces. Mrs. Foley became its first president.

The Reserves' particular job was to look out for girls being molested on Riverside Drive, around the Navy Yard and elsewhere. Frequently Mrs. Foley was compelled to resort to jiu-jitsu to enforce her arrests.

"I could handle 'em all right," she chuckles. "I was a bit of a tough egg in those days."

After the war, between 1920 and 1925, she served on a special service liquor squad, in 1923 became a member of New York's famous "masher squad". Broadway celebrities all knew Mae Foley at sight.

HER MOST dangerous and important assignment was as guardian of women witnesses in the "Lucky" Luciano case, when Thomas E. Dewey was District Attorney.

Because the witnesses were capable of bringing about his conviction, Luciano, head of the New York vice ring, wanted them "bumped off", Mrs. Foley explains. One night, as she was driving her precious cargo to a hide-out in Jackson Heights, she

MAE V. FOLEY

saw in the rear view mirror a car following her. Thinking fast, she turned into a driveway which cut through the block into another street. The quick move threw off her pursuers and Mrs. Foley, instead of going to the hide-out, took her charges to another policewoman's house.

"That's why I'm here today," she smiles. "If we hadn't made it we'd have all been machine-gunned."

But she was not afraid. Fear is not part of Mae Foley's make-up.

The assignment in the Luciano case lasted a year, ended in 1936 with Dewey's first conviction, a life sentence. Again, in 1938, in the Jimmy Hines case that made Dewey governor, Mrs. Foley was assigned to guard the witnesses, this time in a Long Island hideout. Here, her principal antagonist was the notorious "Dutch" Schultz.

PRIOR TO these assignments, Mrs. Foley had studied police methods in Europe and Asia at first hand as the only policewoman to make the New York Police Department's round-the-world cruise in 1934. She followed this up with a Mediterranean cruise in 1935, and in 1938 spent 16 days inside Russia, where she had a chance to see the inside workings of Communism.

During the last war she worked in an undercover squad on espionage and sabotage cases,

losing her identity completely and never going near headquarters. She attended meetings of the German-American Bund until its leader Fritz Kuhn was convicted and the Bund broke up.

Mrs. Foley considers Communism a serious menace today.

"Half the people don't understand what it really means," she says.

According to Mrs. Foley, the policewoman of today needs brains more than brawn.

"Most of them are college graduates," she says. "They must have the technique to know just what to do in any situation."

Mrs. Foley had visited St. Petersburg on a vacation in 1945 and when she retired in 1946, she decided to make this her permanent home. She is living temporarily at 450 Seventh Avenue South.

She has been a widow for 22 years, her late husband having been a Pinkerton man, in charge of all race tracks in New York. She has two daughters and four grandchildren.

Schools Open Today

A two-week Christmas vacation will end this morning for more than 21,000 Pinellas County school children.

Classes resume this morning in public and private schools and St. Petersburg Junior College.

Mae Foley in a story featuring her life and career in the *Tampa Bay Times*. She posed while looking at maps and planning out future trips. (From the *Tampa Bay Times* © 1949 *Tampa Bay Times*, all rights reserved. Used under license.)

Mae didn't even wait for daybreak on January 1. She climbed into her old sedan at one minute after midnight and began to drive south, a free woman. The creaky Ford with the loose springs in the driver's seat didn't even have turn signals. The gearshift promised her it wouldn't put up with any more downshifting at traffic lights. Overall, it promised to be a long, chilly drive for a woman who had to hang one arm out the window to signal her way ahead. But Mae didn't care.

The snowbird was flying away.

CHAPTER 16
LUCK AND LEGACY

It didn't take long for the itching to start, just a little more than four weeks, about the length of time for Mae's typical vacations. By the beginning of February 1946, Mae was bored with her life of leisure. She worried about what was going on at home in New York, in the department, with her grandchildren. And she needed something to do. To feel like she was making a contribution. Mae joined an association for retired police officers, headquartered right there in St. Petersburg, Florida. Of course, they insisted she be called an "honorary member." She was the only woman, after all.[1]

Itchy for action, she couldn't wait for the daffodils to bloom. Mae headed north by the beginning of March, roaring straight up U.S. Route 1, a surprise for her grandchildren. Her daughters weren't surprised at all. "I knew you couldn't stay away from the boys," Grace said with a smile.

"That's true," Mae said, beaming. Johnny held out his arms for Grandma to pick him up.

Florence and her husband continued living at Mae's house, easy enough since she was only there during the summer months. They lived in the basement. That was fine with Mae; she was jealous watching Fred wait on Florence. *Hand and foot*, she muttered to herself. Of course if you could find a man to do all that for you, she reasoned, why not just enjoy it?

He did the shopping, cooking, and ironing and even massaged Florence's feet at night. If Mae was lucky, she only had to see their exaggerated domestic arrangements when they came upstairs to sleep. The basement became their getaway apartment. Fred continued to work in the garment district and Florence also enjoyed having him buy all her clothes. Well, John Foley had called his daughters "princess" when they were little, Mae recalled. Now both were living the dream.

Grace remarried in 1947; she and her new husband, John Carr, made their home in Long Island City. He adopted the boys and had their names changed to Carr. Mae welcomed John with open arms. After all, having married a divorced man herself, she would always say, "I have no business judging anyone else's marriage or their living arrangements."

Florence was never successful in prying the whole story out of Grace. They weren't kids anymore, and Grace wasn't having it. She said just enough to let Florence know that John was the love of her life. That was it as far as Grace was concerned and Florence didn't need to know any more than that.

Florence, though, doted on young Bobby, and Mae had to confess that Johnny was really her favorite. She greatly enjoyed having Grace and her family visit in Florida for a few weeks each winter so she could take the boys to the beach while the parents were off enjoying themselves at the Surf Club tiki bar. When Johnny was six years old, Mae had him flown down to St. Petersburg to meet her in February. Johnny then kept his grandmother company on the long drive back to New York in March. By then, she had a new car, a 1951 Plymouth, big enough to be a boat itself. It had electronic turn signals too, but it never made sense to Mae to push the lever down in order to turn left. It was equally nonsensical to push the lever up to turn right. After a few near hits and misses along the road, she just stuck her arm out the window again. Johnny laughed all the way home.

Back in New York, she still spent time with the boys but she continued all other aspects of her lively social life as well. There were the bunco game sessions, museum visits, and other events with the Democratic ladies club in Jamaica. All those social activities Mae never had time for while working those long hours on the force—she signed up for all of them. Plus, there were her friends from Broadway who visited her in Queens for dinner parties and socializing. Johnny Carr recalled in later years that he met many Broadway stars at his grandmother's home. One or two even babysat the brothers while their parents and grandmother were out for the evening. Not many children can claim that they could call stage and screen star Rita Hayworth their babysitter. "What a life," Mae would comment to them. How lucky they were.

Mae also began to take the boys for summer vacations, ones where they could actually enjoy the great outdoors away from the city, swim, fish, and play without worrying about traffic or crime. She usually scheduled their get-aways in August, and they would pack up the old Plymouth and head north to Vermont for an extended stay at one of the elegant old hotels at Lake Bomoseen, near the towns of Castleton and Hubbardton. The largest lake in Vermont, Bomoseen was home to a number of elegant resorts where guests from New York often stayed for the entire summer, not just a few nights at a time. She'd been there once in the 1930s, a guest of one of her Broadway friends at the famed Algonquin Round Table's private retreat on Neshobe Island. Mae enjoyed the sprightly conversation and repartee with the group of writers, editors, actors, and just plain celebrities, but she wasn't fond of their eccentric host, Alexander Woollcott. He too liked to play cards but had to win at all costs. A few of the guests were a bit odd too. One day, Mae ran across the writer Dorothy Parker, sitting naked under a tree. She learned from the other guests to avoid that particular path.[2]

When she was invited back the following summer, Mae demurred, knowing that guests who were invited back a second time would be offered membership in the expensive club. She didn't return until she traveled with her grandsons following the war. By that time, members of the Round Table gang Mae had met were long gone, taking their hedonistic ways with them.

She would relax on the porch of their hotel, rocking in the white wicker chairs, and chat with the other guests while the boys were out fishing. On rainy afternoons, they would play cards. Mae taught Bobby and Johnny to play one of her favorites, double deck cutthroat pinochle. All the while, she would regale them with stories from her days with the NYPD. Johnny's favorite was one from her days with the Masher Squad, when she slammed the telephone booth door on a pervert's "biggest mistake."

"Slam! Bang! Gramma, you got 'em!" Johnny would crow as his cards flew off the table.

Mae noticed that some of the older ladies at other tables sniffed and turned up their noses at Mae's grandson's reaction. She shrugged. But there were definitely some tables comprised of younger card players who would edge in closer. The stories actually entertained and scandalized the entire assemblage. But by late afternoon, Mae would send the boys off to dress for dinner, and they would enjoy leisurely evenings in the dining room. On the weekends, Florence and Fred and Grace and John might drive up from New York to join them. Sometimes there would be a band and dancing on the veranda. Mae's grandsons remembered she could be coaxed to sing a few of her Irish favorites, including "Danny Boy" and "When Irish Eyes Are Smiling." It was a genteel and pleasant way to pass the late summer days before returning the boys for school.

In stutters and stops, Mae's former department was continuing to evolve and grow too. The NYPD numbered approximately 14,800 officers when Mae's retirement took effect in 1946. By the mid-1950s, that number reached 23,000 and was still growing. New tools, tactics, and technology were on the way too. From handheld radios to the 911 call system, the department was becoming more connected, networked, and responsive. These changes meant graduated changes to police recruitment and education. The City College established classes for prospective officers while the department increased its standards for physical fitness and established special squads for homicide, robbery, and burglary. The department was growing more diverse as well, increasing its number of African Americans and women.[3]

In June 1946, Mae attended the retirement ceremony for her former boss and director of the Women's Police Bureau, Mary Sullivan. At the conclusion of her remarks, Mary gave her final wish: "And may there be many more policewomen—not only in New York but all over the world."[4]

Mary's successor felt the same. Just as other policewomen who had struggled to rise up through the quagmire of repression, prejudice, and discrimination, she knew the same truths they all did. Women could to the work, they made a difference, and they were important to the community in lowering tensions and violent encounters and in protecting the vulnerable.

Theresa M. Scagnelli joined the force two years after Gertrude Schimmel. A former social worker, she could definitely see the connections between her earlier work and community policing. She was a slim young detective in 1949 when she worked undercover as a maid in a hotel where a notorious gambler held court. Each day, she would rifle through his desk after he left and provide incriminating evidence to the district attorney. She later followed the footsteps of Mary Sullivan, commanding the Women's Bureau for ten years. She then became the first woman to be named deputy police commissioner, heading the Bureau of Community Affairs and the Youth Bureau.[5]

Under her married name, Melchionne, she later wrote and spoke frequently on the topic of women in policing. While she espoused many of the same views concerning the typical roles for policewomen as held by her predecessors on the force, she was also a strong advocate for continuing to develop women's roles. She noted, "Traditional concepts of the role and status of women in our society have tended to preclude objective appraisal of the true capabilities of policewomen in the law enforcement field." She emphasized that such views ignored history, empirical studies, and even changes in society. Echoing Mary Sullivan's comments from nearly thirty years earlier, she said that the narrow views of policewomen had "no place in the modern, progressive police agency."[6]

Mae couldn't have agreed more. While she didn't speak out on management topics, her first concern was still for the members of the force. Her first love was still the NYPD. She continued to advocate for her beloved department and supported the Retired Patrolmen's and Policemen's Benevolent Associations in their drive to increase the pensions for widows of police and firemen. Known today as the Police Benevolent Association of the City of New York, it is the largest municipal police union in the world. The association continues to advocate for its members, protecting and advancing their rights and interests. As Mae could appreciate, they keep the traditions of the department, including respect for those who made the ultimate sacrifice in the line of duty.[7] She also had a special place in her heart for the NYPD Policewomen's Endowment Association. She had been a member her entire career, and she continued to advocate for benefits for policewomen.

By 1955, Mae was established as a fixture at city hall, always there to use her voice on behalf of her brothers and sisters on the force. A *Long Island City Star Journal* feature story about her exploits in retirement noted that the mild-mannered grandmother could still "put the fear of God into her opponents."[8]

Not that the mayor's office considered her an opponent. On the contrary, she was the type of advocate who could be counted on to tell the truth and not hold back on issues she deemed important. She started attending public meetings when Robert F. Wagner was mayor. He served three terms, from 1954 to 1965. Wagner was always on the lookout for ways to improve the city and attract both visitors and residents to the metropolis. He was known for building public housing and schools. As a product of public housing herself, Mae more than approved. He also created the City University of New York system and banned housing discrimination based on race or color, and most importantly in Mae's mind, he established the right of city employees to engage in collective bargaining.[9] She liked to think she played a tiny role in helping with that effort on behalf of the NYPD. When asked about her role, she would reply, "Maybe I ought to just sit down and just be a grandmother, but I can't."[10]

When Mayor Wagner didn't see her at one of his meetings that summer, he exclaimed in exaggerated surprise, "What? No Mae Foley?" She made it a point to be there as often as she could. An aide whispered that Mrs. Foley was on a cruise. "Ah, so," the mayor exclaimed. He knew all about her love of travel. And he also knew it wasn't time for her to head south for the winter. It was October 1955.

Earlier in the summer, Mae decided it was finally time to feel the sea breeze again and indulge her fantasies of fame and fortune. She'd given the travel industry long enough to get their act together. Now it was time for the test run. She quickly identified a perfect destination, a ship, and a cabin, booking immediately. That fall, she sailed from New York to Paris on the SS *Ocean Monarch*. The *Monarch* was a new steamship built in 1950, the first postwar ship designed especially for the U.S. market. Mae thought it had beautiful lines and of course she was more than a little pleased with her spacious first-class cabin.[11] Besides Mae, there were over four hundred passengers on board, all of them eager to visit the continent once again. The ship stopped in Bermuda along the way to France, and Mae enjoyed an afternoon stroll along beautiful King's Wharf before returning to the ship.

It was a lovely trip, one well worth the wait. Mae told everyone that. While Air France had begun flying from New York to Paris in 1947, Mae wasn't convinced she was ready to give the new carrier a try. That same year, the RMS *Queen Mary* was relaunched, refitted with air conditioning and three classes of cabins: first class, cabin, and tourist.[12] Mae didn't like the notion of dividing service into different classes; she was waiting for first-class perfection.

With the Paris trip, she found it, all sparkling new and refined. It was the retirement gift she'd waited ten years for. Even though cruise travel continued to decline throughout the 1950s and 1960s, Mae remained devoted to her brand of travel: first-class accommodations, dining, and entertainment, plus a leisurely pace. She was able to recreate the ambience of some of her earlier voyages, lounging in a deck chair, wrapped in a blanket to ward off the spray, and just dozing with the gentle rocking of the ship. That was her idea of perfection.

In the summer of 1956, she took another long cruise, this one to England and Ireland. Mae remained a devotee of the first-class transatlantic crossing despite the increasing popularity of airline travel. She wanted to luxuriate in her travel experiences, not rush them.

Back in New York, she was busy in the borough of Queens too, campaigning in 1956 with John T. (Pat) Clancy and Frank O'Connor to encourage people to vote yes for the city's proposed amendment benefiting police and firemen. Frank O'Connor, the Queens district attorney, was famous in his own right. While in private practice in 1953, O'Connor defended a man falsely accused of armed robbery. The resulting story and book caught the attention of director Alfred Hitchcock, and the movie *The Wrong Man*, starring Henry

Fonda with actor Anthony Quayle playing O'Connor, was released just in time to form the backdrop for the campaign. O'Connor took full advantage of his celebrity status. He'd moved up quickly, going from private practice to the state senate and then elected to serve as district attorney for Queens County. He stayed with the county until 1965, then served as a justice in the Supreme Court for the State of New York.[13]

Borough president Pat Clancy was the giant of the group. Over six feet tall, he towered over both O'Connor and Mae. When people recognized O'Connor during their campaign stops, Mae would inevitably ask him for his autograph, and Clancy would eagerly join in. Then others would crowd around while Clancy and Mae stepped back and exchanged a private laugh.

Clancy was a jovial and outgoing man and, by all accounts, a strong borough president. He'd failed to win his party's nomination for the job in 1955, but in 1959, he was named to serve the remainder of the term of the current borough president, James J. Crisona, when Crisona was elected to the State Supreme Court. Clancy then won the special election in 1959 and ran again in 1961, winning his own term.[14]

Clancy and Mae were mutual fans. In 1961, the borough of Queens recognized Mae by proclaiming her birthday as "Mae Foley Day." The proclamation was a grand creation by the borough president's office. Clancy held a reception in her honor at city hall on July 14 and had the proclamation read aloud. It was all true, well mostly, and somewhat exaggerated, but it was still grand. It read in part that Mae "was New York City's first policewoman, having been appointed October 15, 1923 from the first policewoman's eligibility list."

The lineup of "whereas" statements continued to swell. "She served the Police Department and the city with great ability." Mae could feel herself beginning to blush.

The next series of comments noted that since her retirement on January

1, 1946, she retained the "esteem and affection" of former colleagues and "has made many new friends since she saw the light and moved to Queens many years ago." Mae laughed out loud at that, and the room broke out into applause.

Finally, the proclamation concluded with, "I hereby proclaim Friday July 14th 1961, Mae Foley Day in the Borough of Queens…in token of the esteem and affection in which all who know her hold her."[15]

Borough president Clancy then gave Mae a hug and quick smooch on the cheeks while her family and friends continued to applaud. Noting the tears in her eyes, he handed her his handkerchief, patting her back while grinning at the crowd. It was a heady celebration for the trailblazing policewoman.

Mae's copy of the borough of Queens proclamation honoring her by proclaiming her birthday, July 14, 1961, as Mae Foley Day. ("Proclamation," Borough of Queens, City of New York, July 13, 1961.)

Later that evening, Mae quietly folded the proclamation into her career highlights scrapbook, tucking it in along with newspaper clippings about her exploits on the NYPD, playbills from Broadway shows she'd attended, menus from various cruise ships, and assorted family photos. She turned the page, taking a deep breath. But even at seventy-five, Mae still didn't look her age. Her hair was dark brown, and she only wore glasses to read. And, as the local paper exclaimed breathlessly, she "has all her own teeth."

She didn't act her age either. "Funny thing. When I ask my doctor any questions about my health he just says, 'Don't bother me' and keeps laughing."[16]

Mae Foley had to be doing something right.

CHAPTER 17
A LEGEND REMEMBERED

The lineup of police cars spanned a full mile. There were fire engines too, lights flashing, sirens silent, all part of the solemn procession. The NYPD and the New York Fire Department turned out in force to honor one of their own on December 12, 1967, and a bitter day it was indeed. The temperature that day was 35°F with light winds, but the officers turned out in force to show respect for one of their own.

Mae Foley had passed away four days earlier, on December 8, 1967, at the age of eighty-one, having never once pulled over or taken the slow lane in her approach to life. Her funeral was held at Conway Funeral Home at Northern Boulevard and Eighty-Second Street in Jackson Heights, followed by a funeral mass at Our Lady of Fatima Church.

The massive church was built in 1952, and once it opened, it became Mae's home church. Once, at the conclusion of an early morning service, Mae was walking down the center aisle and happened to look up at the choir loft, just as they began to sing the recessional hymn. She tripped, missed a step on the walkway, and went down on both knees. When she struggled to get up again, Florence called for an ambulance.

The step wasn't marked, and later, when Mae was back home nursing her bruised pride and knees, the bill for the ambulance ride arrived. Her grandson said that several of Mae's friends advised her to sue the parish, but Mae never had any need of attorneys. She had her extensive network of contacts. One call to Borough President Pat Clancy and the bishop gracefully offered to pay for the ambulance ride. He also directed the church to mark that innocuous-looking step in the center aisle as a hazard to guard against any future accidents. Or lawsuits.

Church founder Father Maurice Lenihan had a great deal of respect for Mae Foley and was honored to preside at her funeral on December 12.[1] Her obituary had noted, "Please omit flowers. Masses preferred."[2] Mae wanted it that way. Maybe a few extra masses said on her behalf would secure her a lower number in the line, moving farther along up that long stairway to heaven. If it would help, she'd probably flash her shield as well.

She got her way throughout her life, and she did take chances, sometimes huge risks. But she never took a bribe, and she never looked away when she was faced with wrongdoing. The terms that were applied to her—trailblazer, Amazon, tough, intrepid—were all true. Far more than clichés, those terms fit this woman who made her own way, leaving tracks for the next generation to follow. She owned those titles and exemplified the values and standards a police officer should strive to emulate. Every one. She continued so serve on behalf of her fellow officers even in retirement, living the NYPD motto, "Faithful Unto Death."

Cancer may have taken her, but it never defeated her. Even in her final days as she fought the ravages of the disease, Florence was by her side as she had been throughout her life. Her girls were there for her as she had been for them, and Mae passed peacefully, on her way to rejoin her husband, John.

Her grandsons remember her funeral procession as being four blocks long, all police and firemen paying respects to one of New York City's finest investigators as she was laid to rest. Over two hundred of New York's finest turned out that chilly December day in honor and tribute. These were the individuals who lined up along the streets, while the patrol cars waited patiently for the hearse to move. First there were the policewomen, who had converged from squads and precincts all over the city. While Mae represented an earlier generation, the women serving in the 1960s knew who she was and what she represented. Mae's actions with the Policewomen's Endowment Association were always undertaken on their behalf, ensuring that they were represented when it came to negotiate for better pay and benefits. She fought for them and they knew it.

Then there were the police squads, six to ten deep, lined up in solid formations, representing their precincts, each with their respective flags flying. Mae's old precinct, the 108th, was first, right after the policewomen. Halfway along the lineup, a number of executives from downtown pushed their way to the front and crowded onto the curb. No one wanted to miss the opportunity to say goodbye to Mae Foley.

The officers had begun lining up even before Mae's service started at the church. By the time the bells rang to announce the end of the mass and Mae's children and grandchildren strode out the double doors, they had to pause and gasp. The streets were packed. Officers stood at attention, flags held high. There wasn't a dry eye in the formation as the Pipes and Drums of the Emerald Society of the NYPD played "Amazing Grace" as the hearse with Mae's casket passed by. They saluted her passing, her service, and her example.

Then, just as if she were looking back to request one final song, the band broke into one of her favorites, "Danny Boy."

Policewoman Lillian Reilley, along with three other young policewomen of Irish descent formed the Emerald Society in 1953. Lillian had been with the department just two years at the time but the Society was close to her heart and continued to foster Irish traditions and heritage within the NYPD.[3] The Emerald Society's Pipe and Drums organized in 1960, the first and original pipe band to organize in the United States and played for events in every borough and neighborhood in New York. It was an honor to play for Mae Foley's final ride.[4]

Motorcycles blocked the side streets and patrol cars led the way, and then all joined in again at the entrance to the cemetery. It was a first-class send-off, specially created for a woman whose entire life had been devoted to serving the people of her city.

Mae Foley buried beside her husband John. Her simple headstone gives no indication of her accomplishments in life or her love for her family and her city. Fidelis ad Mortem. (Photo courtesy of the Foley family.)

Young men by then, her grandsons stood stiffly in their new suits and tight shoes, watching with tears in their eyes at the graveside service. "I only wish she could have seen me in uniform," her grandson Johnny said later. He started at the police academy in Greenwood Lake, New York, in January 1968, just six weeks after she passed away. Bobby's eyesight kept him from qualifying as a police officer, but the army permitted him to enlist. Both continued their grandmother's tradition of public service and passed that desire on to succeeding generations. Bobby's son and daughter both joined the NYPD.

CHAPTER 18
TRADITIONS AND PROGRESS

The tradition continues as a family business for many with a history of public service, whether in the military or the police, and Mae's NYPD family has continued to evolve as well. According to the New York City Data Transparency Initiative, by June 2020, 20 percent of NYPD officers were female.[1] The numbers continue to grow, as does the diversity of the force.

New York City Police Academy graduates raise their right hands as they take their oath during their graduation ceremony at Madison Square Garden, Friday, July 1, 2022, in New York. (AP Photo/John Minchillo.)

But as Mae and her contemporaries knew, more work remains. For even as the NYPD reached a milestone of 20 percent female officers on the force in 2020, the department's executives knew they still had a long way to go.

New York University's 30x30 Initiative seeks to end chronic underrepresentation in policing and persuade departments and organizations across the country to commit to reaching at least 30 percent female officers on their rolls by 2030. Given recent media coverage of police brutality, calls to defund the police, and widespread acknowledgment that there are significant issues with a toxic culture in law enforcement as structured today, a greater understanding of the role women play in policing is even more critical.

Research suggests that women use less force than male officers and are named in fewer complaints against police departments. Surveys of public perception confirm that women are generally perceived as more honest, compassionate, and able to create better outcomes for victims of violent crime, and finally, women make fewer discretionary arrests than their male counterparts.[2]

Undoubtedly, Mae Foley and her contemporaries would say, "We could have told you that." In particular, those who came to policing with a background in social work would agree.

Inspector Gertrude Schimmel said as much in 1974. When the president of the Patrolmen's Benevolent Association said that he would campaign to have women removed from foot and squad car patrol because "women lacked the physical and emotional ability to handle violence on patrol duty," Schimmel bristled. She responded that violence was often provoked by overly aggressive male officers. "A woman," she said," can often handle a situation without letting it become violent."[3]

But violence has definitely increased over the years. New York City Transit Police Officer Irma Fran Lozada was shot and killed while attempting to arrest a robbery suspect. The first New York City female officer to die in the line of duty, she had just seven years on the job when her "end of watch" occurred on September 21, 1984.[4]

That violence has also become more random and less predictable. In the past, individuals could take reasonable precautions based on common sense and prior reports, adhering to guidance such as, "Don't walk in the park at night—criminals like darkness. Take the subway at rush hour—criminals don't like witnesses."[5] Now it appears impossible to calculate a margin of safety. Mass shootings, criminals affected by a broad array of mental health issues, and police response that has become increasingly more violent and militarized compound the problem.

Anxiety continues to build in all aspects of conflict resolution. In a 2019 TED Talk, former Newark police chief Ivonne Roman stated, "Much of an officer's day is spent mediating interpersonal conflicts. That's the reality of modern policing."[6] Captain Roman continued, noting that there are over 118 police organizations across the country, and while the NYPD reached a high of 20 percent of female officers assigned in 2020, across the United States, the average number of women in policing by department is still at about 12 percent. That was the number in the NYPD when Mae retired in 1945.

The 30x30 Initiative seeks to have organizations commit to the hiring goal and sign a pledge to make it happen. Of course this is about much more than merely representation. Participating departments must ensure police policies, culture, and commitment to diversity and inclusion all consciously and intentionally support the success of qualified female officers throughout their careers—from hiring to training promotion opportunities, retention, and more. Only then will there be more parity in women at the higher ranks, now stagnating at a mere 3 percent nationwide.

There is also continuing discussion concerning ways in which to provide varied responses to emergency police calls. A Stanford professor recently argued that at least one-third of such calls could safely be directed to "health-focused emergency responders such as mental health professionals, paramedics and social workers," an effort that would require reimagining first responder systems. Such efforts might, he argued, also result in considerable cost savings to a community.[7] It is certainly a concept that merits further study and testing.

In her career, Mae Foley undoubtedly understood the importance of a background in social work and a resulting focus on advocacy for the vulnerable and victimized. Even as Mae served as a sworn officer, she also recognized that increased violence on the part of criminals only ratcheted up higher when confronted by a police policy of "treat 'em rough."

It is only reasonable to expect that Mae would agree on a measured, varied, and multifaceted approach to emergency calls. She would undoubtedly applaud the addition of more women in a greater variety of roles in policing. She would applaud the NYPD for signing the 30x30 pledge in 2021 and continue to support the department's recruiting of women and call for respect for their abilities, service, and ultimately their sacrifices as well.

ACKNOWLEDGMENTS

I am grateful to so many friends and colleagues who helped me wrangle this heretofore unknown story out of obscurity and into the light of day. This is a tale of early policewomen and how they had an impact on the development of policing practices and policy through the early twentieth century. These trailblazers saw it as their duty to protect the vulnerable, the innocent and those at-risk. They demanded and received respect for their contributions. They didn't change history. They made it, carving out a place for themselves and generations of policewomen to follow. And while their contributions were significant, their service was lost, buried in the folds of time and secured there by newer and more pressing problems, lost files, and generations of dwindling interest. Pulling this story out of the shadows was like a treasure hunt, an adventure in tracking down sources, scraps of information, and every reference possible.

I owe a great debt of thanks to Donna and John Carr, who first told me the story of John's grandmother, Detective Mae Foley. I'm so fortunate to have come to know Mae through them, their memories, scrapbooks, and what they saved of her adventures and achievements.

While it's true that the NYPD does not have a historian, the personnel and operational files prior to 1930 lie at the bottom of the East River, and the New York Police Museum shut its doors during the pandemic, I was nonetheless blessed to find so many incredible sources in New York who were helpful and supportive. While I never did locate someone in the New York Police Department to advise me, friends and guides taught me the ways of the city, the location of Madison Square Garden in 1939, what train Mae would have used to go to work and shared what she would have seen as she witnessed the city evolving through the years. I also learned the correct terms to use such as cross streets and not side streets, those minor details that are so important. Still others provided me with insights into the culture and society of the city in the Roaring Twenties and during the Depression that I would never have learned otherwise.

I consulted hundreds of newspapers and magazines in preparing this manuscript, looked at photos in the National Archives and other sources, and visited the New York Public Library for information on police training and the New York City Municipal Library for their records on city employees and salaries.

I'm also thankful for friends with backgrounds in social work, criminal justice, and law enforcement for their views and advice.

Finally, I'm thankful for my agent, Paula Munier, who helped me shape the initial design of this narrative. And my editor Meg Gibbons is a miracle worker, always supportive, positive, and encouraging, which is terrifically important in trying to master a chameleon-like timeline and shifting plot lines. Finally, I'm grateful for the entire team at Sourcebooks for their commitment to telling stories that shouldn't be forgotten.

APPENDIX
FIRSTS AND MORE

1895	Minnie Gertrude Kelly becomes first woman to serve on the Police Board
1897	Isabella Goodwin hired as a matron
1912	Isabella Goodwin becomes first female detective
1915	275 women join the Women's Police Reserve
1918	Mary Hamilton appointed director of the Women's Police Bureau
1918	Mary Sullivan joins the NYPD; later named first female homicide detective
1919	Ten applicants appointed as policewomen: Lillian Leffler, Hortense Thompson, Elizabeth Helms, Lillian Gordon, Sarah Ahearn, Rae Nicoletti, Helen Burns, Mary Cooney, Cora Parchment, and Lawton Bruce; Parchment and Bruce become the first two African American women appointed to the NYPD

1921	Ellen O'Grady appointed deputy commissioner of the Welfare Bureau
1921	Mary Hamilton, Rose Taylor, Ada Barry, Mary McGuire, and Minnie Earnest found the Policewomen's Endowment Association
1922	Edna Pitkin, captain in the Women's Reserve, volunteers to test a bulletproof vest, which is later adopted by the department
1923	Mary "Mae" Foley joins the NYPD, first on the list of eligible candidates
1924	First women named to the Masher Squad: Ellen Newman, Margaret Solon, Anne Murphy, and Catherine Brennan
1924	Mae Foley named to Masher Squad
1925	Mary Sullivan becomes first woman to receive the NYPD Honor Legion
1925	Mary Sullivan named director of the Women's Bureau, holding the post for twenty years
1925	Mae Foley attached to the Nineteenth Precinct, Manhattan, Special Services Squad (Prohibition), becomes first trained policewoman to serve as a detective
1930	Mae Foley assigned to the 108th Precinct, Queens, as detective with the Homicide Squad
1930	Henrietta Additon named sixth deputy police commissioner and director of the Crime Prevention Bureau

"Bureau of Policewomen, 240 Centre Street, Manhattan"
(New York City Civil List, 1933.)

1935   Mary Shanley and four other policewomen become the first women appointed to the Pickpocket Squad

1935–1936   Mae Foley detailed to the staff of District Attorney Thomas Dewey as supervisor of escort and support services for female witnesses in the Lucky Luciano mob trial

1937   Henrietta Additon named director of Welfare Activities for the 1940 World's Fair; later appointed as director of Westfield State Farm, a women's correctional facility

1937   Mae Foley detailed back to the staff of District

Attorney Thomas Dewey as supervisor of escort
and support services for female witnesses in the
Jimmy Hines trial

1939–1940   Mae Foley on undercover assignment to infiltrate
and collect intelligence on the activities of the
German American Bund Nazi movement

1940   Gertrude Schimmel joins the department in the
famous class of 1940; promoted to sergeant along
with Felicia Shpritzer in 1962, and becomes the
first female captain in 1971 and later the first
deputy inspector

1941–1945   Mae Foley assigned to wartime espionage and
sabotage cases for the 108th Precinct

1942   Theresa Scagnelli Melchionne joins the department; later serves as director of the Women's
Bureau for ten years and becomes the first female
deputy police commissioner and director of
Community Affairs and the Youth Bureau

1946   Mae Foley retires from the NYPD

BIBLIOGRAPHY

Newspapers/Television News

"Alban Manor Democrats Hold Card-Bunco Party." *Long Island Sunday Press*, April 3, 1932.

"Amazon of New York." *New York Daily News*, September 25, 1925.

Bartlett, George. "Famous Policewoman from New York Held Her Own with Tough Characters." *Tampa Bay Times*, January 3, 1949.

"Beware of Beauties in Subway Crush." *Brooklyn Daily Eagle*, March 13, 1924. https://bklyn.newspapers.com/image/60011001/?clipping_id=92924057.

"Brooklyn Visitors Are Active in Social Life at Palm Beach." *Brooklyn Daily Eagle*, March 4, 1928. https://bklyn.newspapers.com/image/57569298/.

"Bullets Didn't Even Tickle: Her Vest was Steel." *Buffalo Times*, October 8, 1922. https://www.newspapers.com/clip/54390461edna-pitkin-and-leo-krause-in-the/.

Callahan, Maureen. "Victory Was Ours! NYC Hail VE Day 75 Years Ago." *New York Post*, May 7, 2020. https://nypost.com/2020/05/07/nyc-hailed-v-e-day-75-years-ago/.

Celona, Larry, and Linda Massarella. "Founding Member of NYPD Emerald Society Dies," *New York Post*, November 17, 2017. https://nypost.com/2017/11/19/founding-member-of-nypd-emerald-society-dies/.

"Cruises Added to Honduras." *Brooklyn Daily Eagle*, March 23, 1942. https://bklyn.newspapers.com/image/52618382/?clipping_id=14012144.

Dee, Thomas S., and Jaymes Pyne. "How to Get Cops Out of the Mental-Health

Business." *Wall Street Journal*, July 8, 2022. https://www.wsj.com/articles /how-to-get-cops-out-of-the-mental-health-business-community-response -initiative-police-nonviolent-denver-social-workers-11657297784.

"Detective Ranks Opened to Women." *New York Times*, October 24, 1926. https:// www.nytimes.com/1926/10/24/archives/detective-ranks-opened-to-women -mary-a-sullivan-first-to-gain.html.

"Dinner Planned for Maj. Farrah." *Brooklyn Daily Eagle*, April 22, 1932.

"Efficient Policewoman Theresa Maria Melchionne." *New York Times*, October 29, 1963. https://www.nytimes.com/1963/10/29/archives/efficient-policewoman -theresa-maria-melchionne.html.

"Enright Had Brilliant Career on New York Police Force." *Evening Telegram* (New York), January 15, 1921.

"Entertains Four-O-Boys." *Brooklyn Daily Eagle*, March 12, 1911.

"Facetious Landlords." *Hartford Courant*, February 14, 1854.

"The First Municipal Woman Detective in the World." *New York Times*, March 3, 1912. https://www.newspapers.com/clip/29539671/the-first-municipal-woman -detective-in/.

"First of May—Particulars of the Moving Time." *New York Daily Herald*, May 2, 1852. https://www.loc.gov/resource/sn83030313/1852-05-02/ed-1/?sp=2 &st=image&r=0.494,0.157,0.447,0.183,0.

Fitzsimmons, Emma G., Ali Watkins, and Ashley Southall. "Keechant Sewell to Become First Woman to Lead N.Y.P.D." *New York Times*, December 14, 2021. https://www.nytimes.com/2021/12/14/nyregion/keechant-sewell-nypd -commissioner.html.

"Foley-Evans Wedding in Heights." *Elmhurst Daily Register*, June 28, 1937.

"Girl Companions of 3X Murder Victims Are Back Again at Usual Employments." *Long Island Daily Press*, July 26, 1930.

Hevesi, Dennis. "A Dynamo for Queens: John Thomas (Pat) Clancy." *New York Times*, January 6, 1959. https://www.nytimes.com/1959/01/06/archives/a -dynamo-for-queens-john-thomas-pat-clancy.html.

Hevesi, Dennis. "Frank D. O'Connor, 82, Is Dead." *New York Times*, December 3, 1992. https://www.nytimes.com/1992/12/03/obituaries/frank-d-o-connor -82-is-dead-retired-new-york-appellate-judge.html.

"Higher Ups May be Named in Vice Trial." *Long Island Daily Press*, May 19, 1936.

"Highlights in Mysterious 3X Murders." *North Shore Daily Journal*, June 2, 1936.

"Howard Lindsay, Playwright, Star of 'Life With Father,' Dies." *New York Times*, February 12, 1968. https://www.nytimes.com/1968/02/12/archives/howard -lindsay-playwright-star-of-life-with-father-dies-howard.html.

"Insane Man Hunted in Second Killing." *New York Times*, June 18, 1930. https://
www.nytimes.com/1930/06/18/archives/insane-man-hunted-in-second
-killing-queens-shooting-is-linked-to.html.

Jewish Telegraphic Agency. "Fritz Kuhn Termed 'Threat to Civil Liberties' by
Dewey." *Daily Bulletin*, November 19, 1939. https://www.jta.org/archive
/fritz-kuhn-termed-threat-to-civil-liberties-by-dewey.

Jewish Telegraphic Agency. "Kuhn Embezzlement Trial Begins." *Daily Bulletin*,
November 10, 1939.

"Join the City Patrol Corps: Protect Your Family, Friends, Neighbors and Fellow
Americans." *Long Island Daily Press*, August 24, 1943.

Kilgannon, Corey. "Overlooked No More: Isabella Goodwin, New York City's First
Female Police Detective." *New York Times*, March 13, 2019. https://www
.nytimes.com/2019/03/13/obituaries/isabella-goodwin-overlooked.html.

Klemko, Robert. "This Police Chief Is Hiring Female Officers to Fix 'Toxic Policing.'"
Washington Post, March 27, 2022. https://www.washingtonpost.com
/national-security/interactive/2022/women-police-nebraska/?itid=ap
_robertklemko.

"Kuhn Guilty on All Five Counts." *New York Times*, November 30, 1939. https://
www.nytimes.com/1939/11/30/archives/kuhn-found-guilty-on-all-five
-counts-he-faces-30-years-leader-of.html.

Kwan, Rhoda. "Keechant Sewell Sworn in as NYPD's First Female Police Commissioner."
NBC News, January 1, 2022. https://www.nbcnews.com/news/us-news
/keechant-sewell-sworn-nypds-first-female-police-commissioner-rcna10572.

LaBine, Joseph W. "Mistrial Ruling in Hines Case May Be Setback for Dewey." *Sun*
(Newberry, SC), September 23, 1938.

"Long Island Hosted Nazi Spies in World War II." *Metro Long Island*, April 5, 2011.
https://www.metro.us/long-island-hosted-nazi-spies-in-wwii/.

"Luciano Sentenced to Sing Sing for a Term of 30 to 50 Years." New York *Sun*, June
18, 1936.

"Mae Foley, Famous Policewoman to Retire from Force Dec 31st." *Long Island Star
Journal*, December 22, 1945.

"Mary E. Hamilton Named Director of Policewomen." *Standard Union* (Brooklyn),
March 13, 1924. https://bklyn.newspapers.com/image/544227464/?clipping
_id=92853682.

"Masher Squad Defended." *Evening Star* (Washington, DC), June 8, 1924.

"Masher Squad Makes First Arrest in Brooklyn on 'L.'" *Standard Union* (Brooklyn),
April 4, 1924. https://bklyn.newspapers.com/image/543657457/?clipping
_id=92851724.

"Mayor Hylan Visits Police HQ." *New York Times*, December 7, 1923.

"Member of Masher Squad Assailed in Court by Lawyer." *Brooklyn Daily Eagle*, August 13, 1924.

"More Masher Raids Planned: Curbstone Loafers Infesting Broadway's Sidewalks & Hurling Insults at Women." *New York Evening Telegram*, August 4, 1920.

"'Mother' Sullivan Heads Police Women." *New York Evening Post*, April 28, 1926.

"New York Forms Squad to Snare Male Mashers." *Malone Evening Telegram*, March 18, 1924.

Noonan, Peggy. "Why Crime Is Scarier Now." *Wall Street Journal*, July 7, 2022. https://www.wsj.com/articles/why-crime-scarier-policing-uvalde-elementary-highland-park-shootings-killed-11657228617.

"Obituary for Mae Foley." New York *Daily News*, December 10, 1967.

"Phone Shifts Indicate Moving Day Decline." *Brooklyn Daily Eagle*, October 1, 1930. https://bklyn.newspapers.com/image/57409658/.

"Pistol Packing Mama: Retired in Name Only." *Long Island City Star Journal*, November 17, 1957.

"Police Reserve Ball." *Standard Union* (Brooklyn), January 26, 1919. https://bklyn.newspapers.com/clip/92012851/police-reserve-ball-capt-mae-foley/.

"Police Woman to Retire: Mrs. Mae Foley Began Service in 1923 With 'Masher Squad.'" *New York Times*, December 26, 1945. h ttps://www.nytimes.com/1945/12/26/archives/police-woman-to-retire-mrs-mae-foley-began-service-in-1923-with.html.

"Police Women Get Subway Mashers." *New York American*, December 8, 1923.

"Rev. Maurice Lenihan." *New York Times*, October 19, 1974. https://www.nytimes.com/1974/10/19/archives/rev-maurice-lenihan.html.

Roberts, Sam. "New York 1945; The War Was Ending. Times Square Exploded. Change Was Coming." *New York Times*, July 30, 1995. https://www.nytimes.com/1995/07/30/nyregion/new-york-1945-the-war-was-ending-times-square-exploded-change-was-coming.html.

"Rockefeller Center Is Completed as Its Creator Pleads for Peace." *New York Times*, November 2, 1939. https://www.nytimes.com/1939/11/02/archives/rockefeller-center-is-completed-as-its-creator-pleads-for-peace.html.

Sanderson, Bill. "How Nazi Spies Landed in the Hamptons for Secret Mission." *New York Post*, January 11, 2016. https://nypost.com/2016/06/11/how-nazi-spies-landed-in-the-hamptons-for-secret-mission/.

"Shoplifter Doing Christmas Shopping Early Finds Artificial Hand Useful." *Albany Times Union*, December 16, 1921.

Sulzberger, A. G. "La Guardia's Tough and Incorruptible Police Commissioner." *New*

York Times, November 11, 2009. https://archive.nytimes.com/cityroom .blogs.nytimes.com/2009/11/11/la-guardias-tough-and-incorruptible-police-commissioner/.

"Ten More Women Added to Police: 4 in Brooklyn." *Brooklyn Daily Eagle*, May 27, 1919. https://www.newspapers.com/clip/12572513/cora-parchment-first-african -american/.

"35 Years on Force, Woman to Retire." *New York Times*, April 3, 1946. https://www .nytimes.com/1946/04/03/archives/35-years-on-force-woman-to-retire -mary-agnes-sullivan-has-been.html.

"To Teach Masher Squad Wrestling." *Poughkeepsie Eagle News*, March 13, 1924.

"22,000 Nazis Hold Rally in Garden: Police Check Foes: Scenes as German American Bund Held Its 'Washington Birthday' Rally Last Night." *New York Times*, February 21, 1939. https://www.nytimes.com/1939/02/21/archives/22000 -nazis-hold-rally-in-garden-police-check-foes-scenes-as.html.

"2 Women to Direct Fair Welfare Unit." *New York Times*, April 19, 1937. https:// www.nytimes.com/1937/04/19/archives/2-women-to-direct-fair-welfare -unit-miss-henrietta-additon-and-mrs.html.

"Valentine Extends Greetings to Police." *New York Times*, December 24, 1938. https://www.nytimes.com/1938/12/24/archives/valentine-extends -greetings-to-police-commissioner-compliments-men.html

"Valentine's Ire Stirred by Cop at Vice Trial." New York *Sun*, June 9, 1936.

"Waitress Held in Purse Theft." *Elmhurst Daily Register*, April 7, 1939.

Wells, Micaela. "My History Textbook's Message: Women Don't Matter." *Washington Post*, January 2, 2022.

"Who She Is." *Knickerbocker News*, August 16, 1939.

"Wives of Police Protest Women in Patrol Cars." *New York Times*, June 21, 1974. https://www.nytimes.com/1974/06/21/archives/wives-of-police-protest -women-in-patrol-cars-action-endorsed.html.

"Woman Gun Toter Held on 3 Charges for Grand Jury." *New York Daily News*, September 26, 1925.

"Woman Testifies Against Luciano." *Daily Argus* (Mount Vernon), May 18, 1936.

"Women Detectives Who Get the Crooks." *Brooklyn Daily Eagle*, November 28, 1915.

"Women Police Officers called the Equal of Men." *New York Times*, June 11, 1974. https://www.nytimes.com/1974/06/11/archives/women-police-officers -called-the-equal-of-men.html.

"Women's Police Reserve: Captain Northrup to Organize Corps in 74th Precinct." *Brooklyn Citizen*, June 23, 1918. https://bklyn.newspapers.com /image/544695811/?clipping_id=92013485.

Journals/Magazines

Additon, Henrietta. "Institutional Treatment of Women Offenders." *NPPA Journal* 3, no. 1 (1957): 21–30. https://doi.org/10.1177/0011128757003001.

Bort, Ryan. "When Nazis Took Over Madison Square Garden." *Rolling Stone*, February 18, 2019. https://www.rollingstone.com/politics/politics-news /madison-square-garden-nazis-796197/.

Higgins, Lois. "Historical Background of Policewomen's Service." *Journal of Criminal Law and Criminology* 41, no. 6 (1951): 822–33. https://scholarlycommons .law.northwestern.edu/cgi/viewcontent.cgi?article=3865&context=jclc.

Roman, Ivonne. "Women in Policing: The Numbers Fall Far Short of the Need." *Police Chief*, April 22, 2020. https://www.policechiefmagazine.org/women-in-policing/.

Melchionne, Theresa M. "Current Status and Problems of Women Police." *Journal of Criminal Law and Criminology* 58, no. 2 (1967): 257–60. https://scholarlycommons .law.northwestern.edu/cgi/viewcontent.cgi?article=5454&context=jclc.

Schulz, Dorothy Moses. "A Precinct of Their Own: The New York City Women's Precinct, 1921–1923." *New York History* 85, no. 1 (Winter 2004): 39–64. https://www.jstor.org/stable/23183430.

Books

Annual Report of the Police Department, City of New York, 1923. https://archive.org /details/annual23newy/page/n5/mode/2up.

Barnouw, Erik. *A Tower of Babel: A History of Broadcasting in the United States to 1933.* Oxford: Oxford University Press, 1966.

Bernstein, Arnie. *Swastika Nation: Fritz Kuhn and the Rise and Fall of the German-American Bund.* New York: St. Martin's Press, 2013.

Bren, Paulina. *The Barbizon: The Hotel That Set Women Free.* New York: Simon & Schuster, 2021.

Downey, Patrick. *Bad Seeds in the Big Apple: Bandits, Killers and Chaos in New York City, 1920–1940.* Nashville: Cumberland House, 2008.

Duffin, Allan T. *History in Blue: 160 Years of Women Police, Sheriffs, Detectives, and State Troopers.* Los Angeles: Duffin Creative, 2010.

Edwards, Wallace. *The Real Gangs of New York.* New York: Absolute Crime Books, 2013.

Historical Records and Studies. Vol. IV, parts I and II. New York: United States Catholic Historical Society, 1906.

Janik, Erika. *Pistols and Petticoats: 175 Years of Lady Detectives in Fact and Fiction.* Boston: Beacon Press, 2016.

Johnson, Marilynn S. *Street Justice: A History of Police Violence in New York City.* Boston: Beacon Press, 2003.

Lardner, James, and Thomas Reppetto. *NYPD: A City and Its Police.* New York: Henry Holt and Company, 2000.

Meyer, Robert Jr., ed. *The Stars and Stripes Story of World War II.* New York: David McKay, 1960.

The NYPD: The History and Legacy of the New York City Police Department. n.p.: Charles River Editors, 2019.

O'Neill, Bill. *The Great Book of New York: The Crazy History of New York with Amazing Random Facts & Trivia.* New York: Lak Publishing, 2018.

O'Reilly, Bill, and Martin Dugard. *Killing the Mob: The Fight Against Organized Crime in America.* New York: St. Martin's Press, 2021.

Plowman, Piers, and Stephen J. Card. *Queen of Bermuda and the Furness Bermuda Line.* Bermuda: Bermuda Maritime Press, 2002.

Ruff, Joshua, and Michael Cronin. *Images of America: New York City Police.* Charleston, SC: Arcadia Publishing, 2012.

Scelfo, Julie. *The Women Who Made New York.* New York: Seal Press, 2016.

Slayton, Robert A. *Empire Statesman: The Rise and Redemption of Al Smith.* New York: Simon & Schuster, 2001.

Smith, Richard Norton. *Thomas E. Dewey and His Times.* New York: Simon & Schuster, 1982.

Stickney, Dorothy. *Openings and Closings: Memoir of a Lady of the Theatre.* New York: Doubleday, 1979.

Strausbaugh, John. *Victory City: A History of New York and New Yorkers During World War II.* New York: Hachette Book Group, 2018.

Sullivan, Mary. *My Double Life: The Story of a New York Policewoman.* New York: Farrar & Rinehart, 1938.

Thompson, Donald H. *Lake Bomoseen: The Story of Vermont's Largest Little-Known Lake.* Charleston: History Press, 2009.

Walsh, Marie de Lourdes. *The Sisters of Charity of New York 1809–1959.* New York: Fordham University Press, Vol. II, 1960.

Whalen, Bernard J., Philip Messing, and Robert Mladinich. *Undisclosed Files of the Police: Cases from the Archives of the NYPD from 1831 to the Present.* New York: Black Dog & Leventhal, 2016.

Pamphlets

"Bureau of Policewomen, 240 Centre Street, Manhattan," New York City Civil List, 1933.

Kelly, Raymond W. "The History of New York City Police Department." U.S. Department of Justice, 1994. https://www.ojp.gov/pdffiles1/Digitization /145539NCJRS.pdf.

Police Academy (Institute of Police Science) Training Manual. "The New York Police Academy: Enter to Learn... Go Forth to Serve," Police Department, City of New York, 1933

Plays

Lindsay, Howard, and Russel Crouse. *Life with Father*. New York: Alfred A. Knopf, 1940.

Life with Father, The Playbill, New York Theatre Program Corporation, 1942.

Websites/Blogs

Atiya, Alexander. "Three Million Dead in Queens: A Short History of Calvary Cemetery." New York Moon. February 2008. http://nymoon.com/pubs /undertone/dead/.

Backes, Aaron D. "Robert F. Wagner Jr.—History of New York City Mayors." Classic New York History. January 20, 2021. https://classicnewyorkhistory.com /robert-f-wagner-jr-history-of-new-york-city-mayors/.

"The Bomb Squad." PoliceNY. Accessed September 29, 2022. http://www.policeny .com/bomb1.html.

Brouwer, Norman. "Defending New York City's Eastern Gateway: A History of Fort Totten on Willets Point." Bayside Historical Society. September 6, 2016. https://web.archive.org/web/20160906012609/http://www.hoflink .com/~bayside/brouwer.html.

Brumfeld, Dale M. "July 4, 1940 World's Fair Bombing Still Unsolved." Lessons from History. September 28, 2019. https://medium.com/lessons-from-history /july-4–1940-worlds-fair-bombing-still-unsolved-ae2132e25661.

Carlson, Jen. "Flashback: NYC's War Time Dimouts." Gothamist. June 13, 2011. https://gothamist.com/arts-entertainment/flashback-nycs-war-time-dimouts.

Cavanaugh, Mariah. "Eunice Carter: The Unlikely Hero Who Brought Down the Mob." St. Mary's University Research Scholars. March 22, 2019. https:// stmuscholars.org/eunice-carter-the-unlikely-hero-who-brought-down-the-mob/.

"Chronological List of Brooklyn Parishes, 1822–2008." Diocese of Brooklyn. 2012. https://dioceseofbrooklyn.org/wp-content/uploads/2012/10/chronological _list_brooklyn_parish_school_2012.pdf.

Cobb, Geoffrey. "Mayor Walker Charming and Corrupt." *Irish Echo*. January 31, 2022. https://www.irishecho.com/2022/1/new-york-s-mayor-walker-charming-and-corrupt.

"Current NYPD Members of Service." NYC Civilian Complaint Review Board Data Transparency Initiative. Accessed September 30, 2022. https://www1.nyc.gov/site/ccrb/policy/data-transparency-initiativemos.page.

"Did the British Plant A Bomb at 1940 World's Fair to Kill 2 NYPD Officers and Bring the U.S. into World War II?" DailyMail.com. July 17, 2017. https://www.dailymail.co.uk/news/article-4703958/Did-British-plant-bomb-World-s-Fair-1940.html

Fitzpatrick, Kevin C. "10 Traces of World War I You Can Still Find in NYC on the Centennial Anniversary." Untapped New York. March 21, 2017. https://untappedcities.com/2017/03/21/10-traces-of-world-war-i-you-can-still-find-in-nyc-on-the-centennial-anniversary/4/?displayall=true.

Fox, Deanna. "Historic Carousels in Upstate New York." NYUp.com. May 5, 2016. https://www.newyorkupstate.com/attractions/2016/05/historic_carousels_in_upstate_new_york_where_to_ride_a_piece_of_history_photos.html.

"The Great White Way." Spotlight on Broadway. Accessed September 28, 2022. https://www.spotlightonbroadway.com/the-great-white-way-0.

"History of Aqueduct." New York Racing Authority. 2022. https://www.nyra.com/aqueduct/about/history-of-aqueduct.

"History of Cruising." Cruise Jobs. November 6, 2012. https://cruise.jobs/history-of-cruising/.

"The History of Women in the NYPD." Policewoman's Endowment Association. 2018. https://web.archive.org/web/20200627203512/http://nypdpea1.org/index.php/history/.

Holzwarth, Larry. "German Sabotage and Espionage in the United States during WWII." History Collection. December 14, 2019. https://historycollection.com/german-sabotage-and-espionage-in-the-united-states-during-wwii/.

"How to Play Bunco? Rules & Strategies." Bar Games 101, December 15, 2020. https://bargames101.com/bunco-rules/.

"*Invisible* Chronicles the Life of Eunice Carter, A Pioneering Black Woman Prosecutor." Fordham News. February 22, 2019. https://news.fordham.edu/fordham-magazine/invisible-chronicles-the-life-of-eunice-carter-a-pioneering-black-woman-prosecutor/.

Keck, Zachary. "World War II: Did the Nazis Sabotage a Ship in New York?" Center for the National Interest. November 15, 2020. https://nationalinterest.org/blog/reboot/world-war-ii-did-nazis-sabotage-ship-new-york-172574.

Kelly, Kerry C. "The Volstead Act." National Archives. Last updated February 24, 2017. https://www.archives.gov/education/lessons/volstead-act.

"Kungsholm 1928–1941." A Tribute to the Swedish American Line. Accessed September 29, 2022. http://www.salship.se/kung1.php.

"Life With Father." Internet Broadway Database. Accessed September 30, 2022. https://www.ibdb.com/broadway-show/life-with-father-5379.

"Part V: Life During Wartime… From Nazi Spies to Bigamous Bride." FBI Commemorative World War II History television series. September 28, 2005. https://archives.fbi.gov/archives/news/stories/2005/september/history _092805.

"The Lost Church of Saint Gabriel." Daytonian in Manhattan. May 22, 2017. https://daytoninmanhattan.blogspot.com/2017/05/the-lost-church-of-st -gabriel-310-east.html.

Marques, Stuart. "Prohibition." NYC Department of Records & Information Services. March 8, 2019. https://www.archives.nyc/blog/2019/3/8/prohibition.

McCarthy, Andy. "Genealogy Tips: New York City Cops in the City Record." New York Public Library. August 18, 2017. https://www.nypl.org/blog/2017/08/18 /researching-nypd-city-record.

McNamara, Robert. "Theodore Roosevelt and the New York Police Department." ThoughtCo. June 19, 2019. https://www.thoughtco.com/theodore-roosevelt -ny-police-department-1773515.

"Nazi Saboteurs and George Dasch." FBI History. Accessed September 30, 2022. https://www.fbi.gov/history/famous-cases/nazi-saboteurs-and-george -dasch.

"New York's Scotland Yard: Old NYPD Headquarters 240 Centre Street." Infamous New York. April 25, 2015. https://infamousnewyork.com/2015/04/25/new -yorks-scotland-yard-old-nypd-headquarters-240-centre-street/.

Nonko, Emily. "The 100-Year History of New York's Settlement House Collective." 6sqft. November 22, 2019. https://www.6sqft.com/the-100-year-history-of -new-yorks-settlement-house-collective/.

Pipes and Drums of the Emerald Society of the NYPD. Accessed September 30, 2022. https://nypdpipesanddrums.com/.

"Police Officer Irma Fran Lozada." Officer Down Memorial Page. Accessed September 30, 2022. https://www.odmp.org/officer/8301-police-officer-irma -fran-lozada.

"PPF History." New York City Police Pension Fund. Accessed September 30, 2022. https://www1.nyc.gov/html/nycppf/html/home/home.shtml.

"President Roosevelt Opens 1939 New York World's Fair." American History

TV. April 30, 1939. https://www.c-span.org/video/?319178–1/president
-roosevelt-opens-1939-york-worlds-fair.

"Prohibition." History. Last updated August 12, 2022. https://www.history.com
/topics/roaring-twenties/prohibition.

Roman, Ivonne. "How Policewomen Make Communities Safer." TED Talk. July
30, 2019. https://www.ted.com/talks/ivonne_roman_how_policewomen
_make_communities_safer.

"Sherlock Holmes in Skirts: The World's First Policewomen." BBC History Extra.
November 2020. https://www.historyextra.com/period/20th-century/world
-first-policewomen-who-when-female-police/.

Smyth, Ted. "New York's Gas House District." Resurrecting the Ethnic Village. 2018.
https://ethnic-village.org/the-gas-house-district/.

"Surrogate's Court, New York County: Historical Information." New York Unified
Court System. Accessed September 28, 2022. https://ww2.nycourts.gov
/courts/1jd/surrogates/historical.shtml.

"Texas Guinan Biography." Internet Movie Database. Accessed September 28, 2022.
https://www.imdb.com/name/nm0347345/.

30x30 Initiative: Advancing Women in Policing. Accessed September 30, 2022.
https://30x30initiative.org/.

"Thomas Dewey." Mob Museum. Accessed September 29, 2022. https://
themobmuseum.org/notable_names/thomas-dewey/.

Tierney, John J. "St. Gabriel Has Left the Building." *Currach* (blog). April 27, 2011.
https://currach.johnjtierney.com/2011/04/st-gabriel-has-left-the-building/.

"VJ Day." National World War II Museum. Accessed September 30, 2022. https://
www.nationalww2museum.org/war/articles/v-j-day.

"Welcome to the History of the Honor Legion." NYPD Honor Legion. Accessed
September 28, 2022. http://nypdhl.com/history.htm.

"Who We Are." Police Benevolent Association of the City of New York. Accessed
September 30, 2022. http://nycpba.org/about-the-pba/who-we-are/.

Other

"Proclamation." Borough of Queens, City of New York. July 13, 1961.

NOTES

Introduction

1   "Pistol Packing Mama: Retired in Name Only," *Long Island City Star Journal*, November 17, 1957.

2   Andy McCarthy, "Genealogy Tips: New York Cops in the City Record," New York Public Library, August 18, 2017, https://www.nypl.org/blog/2017/08/18 /researching-nypd-city-record.

3   Ivonne Roman, "Women in Policing: The Numbers Fall Far Short of the Need," *Police Chief*, April 22, 2020, https://www.policechiefmagazine.org/women-in-policing/.

4   Corey Kilgannon, "Overlooked No More: Isabella Goodwin, New York City's First Female Police Detective," *New York Times*, March 13, 2019, https://www .nytimes.com/2019/03/13/obituaries/isabella-goodwin-overlooked.html.

5   Emma G. Fitzsimmons, Ali Watkins, and Ashley Southall, "Keechant Sewell to Become First Woman to Lead N.Y.P.D.," *New York Times*, December 14, 2021, https://www.nytimes.com/2021/12/14/nyregion/keechant-sewell-nypd -commissioner.html.

6   Robert Klemko, "This Police Chief Is Hiring Female Officers to Fix 'Toxic Policing,'" *Washington Post*, March 27, 2022, https://www.washingtonpost.com /national-security/interactive/2022/women-police-nebraska/?itid=ap _robertklemko.

7   Klemko. "Police Chief."

Chapter 1. Born Lucky, Growing Up Tough

1   "Mae Foley, Famous Policewoman to Retire from Force Dec 31st," *Long Island Star Journal*, December 22, 1945.

2   Ted Smyth, "New York's Gas House District," Resurrecting the Ethnic Village (website), 2018, https://ethnic-village.org/the-gas-house-district/.

3   "Detective Ranks Opened to Women," *New York Times*, October 24, 1926, https://www.nytimes.com/1926/10/24/archives/detective-ranks-opened-to-women-mary-a-sullivan-first-to-gain.html.

4   "The History of Women in the NYPD," Policewomen's Endowment Association, 2018, https://web.archive.org/web/20200627203512/http://nypdpea1.org/index.php/history/.

5   Raymond W. Kelly, "The History of New York City Police Department," U.S. Department of Justice, 1994, https://www.ojp.gov/pdffiles1/Digitization/145539NCJRS.pdf.

6   Wallace Edwards, *The Real Gangs of New York* (New York: Absolute Crime Books, 2013), 15.

7   Paulina Bren, *The Barbizon: The Hotel That Set Women Free* (New York: Simon & Schuster, 2021), 19.

8   Robert McNamara, "Theodore Roosevelt and the New York Police Department," ThoughtCo, June 19, 2019, https://www.thoughtco.com/theodore-roosevelt-ny-police-department-1773515.

9   Bren, *Barbizon*, 19.

10 Marie de Lourdes Walsh, *The Sisters of Charity of New York 1809–1959* (New York: Fordham University Press, Vol. II, 1960), 38.

11 John J. Tierney, "St. Gabriel Has Left the Building," *Currach* (blog), April 27, 2011, https://currach.johnjtierney.com/2011/04/st-gabriel-has-left-the-building/.

12 *The NYPD: The History and Legacy of the New York City Police Department* (n.p.: Charles River Editors, 2019), 42.

Chapter 2. Foot in the Door

1   George Bartlett, "Famous Policewoman From New York Held Her Own With Tough Characters," *Tampa Bay Times*, January 3, 1949.

2   Emily Nonko, "The 100-Year History of New York's Settlement House Collective," 6sqft, November 22, 2019, https://www.6sqft.com/the-100-year-history-of-new-yorks-settlement-house-collective/.

3   "Surrogate's Court, New York County: Historical Information," New York Unified Court System, accessed September 28, 2022, https://ww2.nycourts.gov/courts/1jd/surrogates/historical.shtml.

4   "New York's Spanish-American War Rosters," New York State Military Museum and Veterans Research Center, accessed September 28, 2022, https://museum .dmna.ny.gov/unit-history/conflict/spanish-american-war-1898/new-yorks -spanish-american-war-rosters.

5   Deanna Fox, "Historic Carousels in Upstate New York," NYUp.com, May 5, 2016, https://www.newyorkupstate.com/attractions/2016/05/historic_carousels_in _upstate_new_york_where_to_ride_a_piece_of_history_photos.html.

6   "The Great White Way," Spotlight on Broadway, accessed September 28, 2022, https://www.spotlightonbroadway.com/the-great-white-way-0.

7   "Women Detectives Who Get the Crooks," Brooklyn Daily Eagle, November 28, 1915.

8   Kilgannon, "Overlooked No More."

9   "Women Detectives Who Get the Crooks."

10 "The First Municipal Woman Detective in the World," New York Times, March 3, 1912. https://www.newspapers.com/clip/29539671/the-first-municipal -woman-detective-in/.

11 Kilgannon, "Overlooked No More."

Chapter 3. A Shot of Progress

1   Allan T. Duffin, History in Blue: 160 Years of Women Police, Sheriffs, Detectives, and State Troopers (Los Angeles: Duffin Creative, 2010), 44.

2   Duffin, History in Blue, 59.

3   Kevin C. Fitzpatrick, "10 Traces of World War I You Can Still Find in NYC on the Centennial Anniversary," Untapped New York, March 21, 2017, https:// untappedcities.com/2017/03/21/10-traces-of-world-war-i-you-can-still-find -in-nyc-on-the-centennial-anniversary/4/?displayall=true.

4   Mary Sullivan, My Double Life: The Story of a New York Policewoman (New York: Farrar & Rinehart, 1938), 134.

5   Duffin, History in Blue, 62.

6   "Mae Foley, Famous Policewoman."

7   Bartlett, "Famous Policewoman."

8   Erika Janik, Pistols and Petticoats: 175 Years of Lady Detectives in Fact and Fiction (Boston: Beacon Press, 2016), 110.

9   Duffin, History in Blue, 63.

10 "Women's Police Reserve: Captain Northrup to Organize Corps in 74th Pre-cinct," Brooklyn Citizen, June 23, 1918, https://bklyn.newspapers.com/image /544695811/?clipping_id=92013485.

11 Janik, Pistols and Petticoats, 119.

12 Joshua Ruff and Michael Cronin, *Images of America: New York City Police* (Charleston, SC: Arcadia Publishing, 2012), 52.

13 Duffin, *History in Blue*, 60.

14 "Police Reserve Ball," *Standard Union* (Brooklyn), January 26, 1919, https://bklyn .newspapers.com/clip/92012851/police-reserve-ball-capt-mae-foley/.

15 "Ten More Women Added to Police: 4 in Brooklyn," *Brooklyn Daily Eagle*, May 27, 1919, https://www.newspapers.com/clip/12572513/cora-parchment-first -african-american/.

16 "Ten More Women."

Chapter 4. Package Deal

1 "History of Aqueduct," New York Racing Authority, 2022, https://www.nyra.com /aqueduct/about/history-of-aqueduct.

2 "First Municipal Woman Detective."

3 Bill O'Neill, *The Great Book of New York: The Crazy History of New York with Amazing Random Facts & Trivia* (New York: Lak Publishing, 2018), 131.

4 "Prohibition," History, last updated August 12, 2022, https://www.history.com /topics/roaring-twenties/prohibition.

5 Bren, *Barbizon*, 32.

6 James Lardner and Thomas Reppetto, *NYPD: A City and Its Police* (New York: Henry Holt, 2000), 198.

7 "Bullets Didn't Even Tickle: Her Vest Was Steel," *Buffalo Times*, October 8, 1922, https://www.newspapers.com/clip/54390461/edna-pitkin-and-leo-krause-in-the/.

8 Lois Higgins, "Historical Background of Policewomen's Service," *Journal of Criminal Law and Criminology* 41, no. 6 (1951): 822–33, https://scholarlycommons.law .northwestern.edu/cgi/viewcontent.cgi?article=3865&context=jclc.

9 Dorothy Moses Schulz, "A Precinct of Their Own: The New York City Women's Precinct, 1921–1923," *New York History* 85, no. 1 (Winter 2004): 39–64, https://www.jstor.org/stable/23183430.

10 Duffin, *History in Blue*, 74.

11 *Annual Report of the Police Department, City of New York*, 1923, 124, https:// archive.org/details/annual23newy/page/n5/mode/2up.

12 *Annual Report of the Police Department*, 130.

Chapter 5. Cake Eaters and Mashers

1 "Mayor Hylan Visits Police HQ," *New York Times*, December 7, 1923.

2   "New York Forms Squad to Snare Male Mashers," *Malone Evening Telegram*, March 18, 1924.

3   Robert A. Slayton, *Empire Statesman: The Rise and Redemption of Al Smith* (New York: Simon & Schuster, 2001), 122.

4   "To Teach Masher Squad Wrestling," *Poughkeepsie Eagle News*, March 13, 1924.

5   "Mary E. Hamilton Named Director of Policewomen," *Standard Union* (Brooklyn), March 13, 1924, https://bklyn.newspapers.com/image/544227464/?clipping_id=92853682.

6   "Beware of Beauties in Subway Crush," *Brooklyn Daily Eagle*, March 13, 1924, https://bklyn.newspapers.com/image/60011001/?clipping_id=92924057.

7   "Police Women Get Subway Mashers," *New York American*, December 8, 1923.

8   "Masher Squad Makes First Arrest in Brooklyn on 'L,'" *Standard Union* (Brooklyn), April 4, 1924, https://bklyn.newspapers.com/image/543657457/?clipping_id=92851724.

9   "Mae Foley, Famous Policewoman."

10   "Masher Squad Defended," *Evening Star* (Washington, DC), June 8, 1924.

11   "Enright Had Brilliant Career on New York Police Force," *Evening Telegram* (New York), January 15, 1921.

12   Duffin, *History in Blue*, 77.

13   "Detective Ranks Opened to Women."

14   "'Mother' Sullivan Heads Police Women," *New York Evening Post*, April 28, 1926.

15   "Sherlock Holmes in Skirts: The World's First Policewomen," BBC History Extra, November 2020, https://www.historyextra.com/period/20th-century/world-first-policewomen-who-when-female-police/.

Chapter 6. The Mad House

1   Duffin, *History in Blue*, 79.

2   "Welcome to the History of the Honor Legion," NYPD Honor Legion, accessed September 28, 2022, http://nypdhl.com/history.htm.

3   Sullivan, *My Double Life*, 296.

4   Duffin, *History in Blue*, 79.

5   Geoffrey Cobb, "Mayor Walker Charming and Corrupt," *Irish Echo*, January 31, 2022, https://www.irishecho.com/2022/1/new-york-s-mayor-walker-charming-and-corrupt.

6   Stuart Marques, "Prohibition," NYC Department of Records & Information Services, March 8, 2019, https://www.archives.nyc/blog/2019/3/8/prohibition.

7   "Texas Guinan Biography," IMDb, accessed September 28, 2022, https://www
     .imdb.com/name/nm0347345/bio.

8   Bren, *Barbizon*, 36–37.

9   Marilynn S. Johnson, *Street Justice: A History of Police Violence in New York City*
     (Boston: Beacon Press, 2003), 120.

10   Patrick Downey, *Bad Seeds in the Big Apple: Bandits, Killers and Chaos in New
     York City, 1920–1940* (Nashville: Cumberland House, 2008), 12.

11   "Mae Foley, Famous Policewoman."

12   "Woman Gun Toter Held on 3 Charges for Grand Jury," *New York Daily News*,
     September 26, 1925.

13   "Amazon of New York," *New York Daily News*, September 25, 1925.

14   "Woman Gun Toter."

Chapter 7. Wonder Years

1   Sullivan, *My Double Life*, 140.

2   Kelly, "History of New York City Police Department."

3   "New York's Scotland Yard: Old NYPD Headquarters 240 Centre Street," Infa-
     mous New York, April 25, 2015, https://infamousnewyork.com/2015/04/25
     /new-yorks-scotland-yard-old-nypd-headquarters-240-centre-street/.

4   *New York Police Academy: Enter to Learn… Go Forth to Serve* (New York: New
     York Police Department, 1933), 19.

5   "Shoplifter Doing Christmas Shopping Early Finds Artificial Hand Useful,"
     Times Union (Albany), December 16, 1921.

6   Sullivan, *My Double Life*, 192–93.

7   Alexander Atiya, "Three Million Dead in Queens: A Short History of Cal-
     vary Cemetery," New York Moon, February 2008, http://nymoon.com/pubs
     /undertone/dead/.

8   Bren, *Barbizon*, 47.

9   Kelly, "History of New York City Police Department."

10   O'Neill, *Great Book of New York*, 29.

Chapter 8. Live Bait

1   "First of May—Particulars of the Moving Time," *New York Daily Herald*, May 2,
     1852, https://www.loc.gov/resource/sn83030313/1852-05-02/ed-1/?sp=2&st
     =image&r=0.494,0.157,0.447,0.183,0.

2   "Facetious Landlords," *Hartford Courant*, February 14, 1854.

3   "Phone Shifts Indicate Moving Day Decline," *Brooklyn Daily Eagle*, October 1, 1930, https://bklyn.newspapers.com/image/57409658/.

4   Erik Barnouw, *A Tower of Babel: A History of Broadcasting in the United States to 1933* (Oxford: Oxford University Press, 1966), 110.

5   Lardner and Reppetto, *NYPD*, 224.

6   "Highlights in Mysterious 3X Murders," *North Shore Daily Journal*, June 2, 1936.

7   "Insane Man Hunted in Second Killing," *New York Times*, June 18, 1930, https://www.nytimes.com/1930/06/18/archives/insane-man-hunted-in-second-killing-queens-shooting-is-linked-to.html.

8   "Mae Foley, Famous Policewoman."

9   "Girl Companions of 3X Murder Victims Are Back Again at Usual Employments," *Long Island Daily Press*, July 26, 1930.

Chapter 9. Rhythm and Blues

1   Duffin, *History in Blue*, 70.

2   Ruff and Cronin, *New York City Police*, 67.

3   Sullivan, *My Double Life*, 296.

4   "How to Play Bunco? Rules & Strategies," Bar Games 101, December 15, 2020, https://bargames101.com/bunco-rules/.

5   "Alban Manor Democrats Hold Card-Bunco Party," *Long Island Sunday Press*, April 3, 1932.

6   "Alban Manor Democrats."

7   Andy McCarthy, "Genealogy Tips: New York City Cops in The City Record," New York Public Library, Aug 18, 2017, https://www.nypl.org/blog/2017/08/18/researching-nypd-city-record.

8   Ruff and Cronin, *New York City Police*, 77.

9   "History of Women in the NYPD."

10 Bren, *Barbizon*, 52.

11 Julie Scelfo, *The Women Who Made New York* (New York: Seal Press, 2016), 146.

12 Duffin, *History in Blue*, 104.

13 Lardner and Reppetto, *NYPD*, 223.

14 Lardner and Reppetto, *NYPD*, 224.

15 Johnson, *Street Justice*, 121.

16 Johnson, *Street Justice*, 121–22.

17 "Thomas Dewey," Mob Museum, accessed September 29, 2022, https://themobmuseum.org/notable_names/thomas-dewey/.

Chapter 10. Trials and Tribulations

1   "*Invisible* Chronicles the Life of Eunice Carter, A Pioneering Black Woman Prosecutor," Fordham News, February 22, 2019, https://news.fordham.edu/fordham-magazine/invisible-chronicles-the-life-of-eunice-carter-a-pioneering-black-woman-prosecutor/.

2   "Thomas Dewey."

3   Mariah Cavanaugh, "Eunice Carter: The Unlikely Hero Who Brought Down the Mob," St. Mary's University Research Scholars, March 22, 2019, https://stmuscholars.org/eunice-carter-the-unlikely-hero-who-brought-down-the-mob/.

4   Cavanaugh, "Eunice Carter."

5   Richard Norton Smith, *Thomas E. Dewey and His Times* (New York: Simon & Schuster, 1982), 195.

6   "Woman Testifies Against Luciano," *Daily Argus* (Mount Vernon), May 18, 1936.

7   "Higher Ups May Be Named in Vice Trial," *Long Island Daily Press*, May 19, 1936.

8   Bartlett, "Famous Policewoman."

9   "Luciano Sentenced to Sing Sing for a Term of 30 to 50 Years," *Sun*, June 18, 1936.

10 "Valentine's Ire Stirred by Cop at Vice Trial," *Sun*, June 9, 1936.

11 "Educational Characteristics of the Population by Age: 1940," United States Census Bureau, December 23, 1943, https://www.census.gov/library/publications/1943/demo/p19-4.html.

12 "Foley-Evans Wedding in Heights," *Elmhurst Daily Register*, June 28, 1937.

13 "Rockefeller Center Is Completed as Its Creator Pleads for Peace," *New York Times*, November 2, 1939, https://www.nytimes.com/1939/11/02/archives/rockefeller-center-is-completed-as-its-creator-pleads-for-peace.html.

Chapter 11. Chasing Good Times

1   "History of Women in the NYPD."

2   "Kungsholm 1928–1941," A Tribute to the Swedish American Line (website), accessed September 29, 2022, http://www.salship.se/kung1.php.

3   Dorothy Stickney, *Openings and Closings: Memoir of a Lady of the Theatre* (New York: Doubleday, 1979), 111.

4   Stickney, *Openings and Closings*, 111.

5   "Mae Foley, Famous Policewoman."

6   Stickney, *Openings and Closings*, 113.

7   Bartlett, "Famous Policewoman."

8   "Howard Lindsay, Playwright, Star of 'Life with Father,' Dies," *New York Times*,

February 12, 1968, https://www.nytimes.com/1968/02/12/archives/howard
-lindsay-playwright-star-of-life-with-father-dies-howard.html.

9   "Thomas Dewey."

10 Smith, *Dewey and His Times*, 250.

11 Joseph W. LaBine, "Mistrial Ruling in Hines Case May be Setback for Dewey,"
Sun (Newberry, SC), September 23, 1938.

12 "Valentine Extends Greetings to Police," *New York Times*, December 24, 1938,
https://www.nytimes.com/1938/12/24/archives/valentine-extends-greetings
-to-police-commissioner-compliments-men.html.

13 Atkinson Brooks, introduction to *Life with Father*, by Howard Lindsay and
Russel Crouse (New York: Alfred A. Knopf, 1940), viii.

Chapter 12. Undercover and Out of Sight

1   Bren, *Barbizon*, 71.

2   "President Roosevelt Opens 1939 New York World's Fair," American History TV,
April 30, 1939, https://www.c-span.org/video/?319178–1/president
-roosevelt-opens-1939-york-worlds-fair.

3   Johnson, *Street Justice*, 179.

4   Arnie Bernstein, *Swastika Nation: Fritz Kuhn and the Rise and Fall of the German-
American Bund* (New York: St. Martin's Press, 2013), 179.

5   Bernstein, *Swastika Nation*, 2.

6   Bernstein, *Swastika Nation*, 2.

7   Ryan Bort, "When Nazis Took Over Madison Square Garden," *Rolling Stone*, February 18, 2019, https://www.rollingstone.com/politics/politics-news/madison
-square-garden-nazis-796197/.

8   "22,000 Nazis Hold Rally in Garden: Police Check Foes: Scenes as German American Bund Held Its 'Washington Birthday' Rally Last Night," *New York Times*,
February 21, 1939, https://www.nytimes.com/1939/02/21/archives/22000
-nazis-hold-rally-in-garden-police-check-foes-scenes-as.html.

9   "Waitress Held in Purse Theft," *Elmhurst Daily Register*, April 7, 1939.

10 "Who She Is," *Knickerbocker News*, August 16, 1939.

11 Jewish Telegraphic Agency, "Fritz Kuhn Termed 'Threat to Civil Liberties' by
Dewey," *Daily Bulletin*, November 19, 1939, https://www.jta.org/archive/fritz
-kuhn-termed-threat-to-civil-liberties-by-dewey.

12 "Kuhn Found Guilty on All Five Counts," *New York Times*, November 30, 1939,
https://www.nytimes.com/1939/11/30/archives/kuhn-found-guilty-on-all
-five-counts-he-faces-30-years-leader-of.html.

13 "2 Women to Direct Fair Welfare Unit," *New York Times*, April 19, 1937, https://www.nytimes.com/1937/04/19/archives/2-women-to-direct-fair-welfare-unit-miss-henrietta-additon-and-mrs.html.

14 Henrietta Additon, "Institutional Treatment of Women Offenders," *NPPA Journal* 3, no. 1 (1957): 21–30, https://doi.org/10.1177/0011128757003001.

15 "Did the British Plant A Bomb at 1940 World's Fair to Kill 2 NYPD Officers and Bring the U.S. into World War II?" DailyMail.com, July 17, 2017, https://www.dailymail.co.uk/news/article-4703958/Did-British-plant-bomb-World-s-Fair-1940.html

16 Bernard J. Whalen, Philip Messing, and Robert Mladinich, *Undisclosed Files of the Police: Cases from the Archives of the NYPD from 1831 to the Present* (New York: Black Dog & Leventhal, 2016), 125–27.

17 Lardner and Reppetto, *NYPD*, 190.

18 "The Bomb Squad," PoliceNY, accessed September 29, 2022, http://www.policeny.com/bomb1.html.

Chapter 13. War Again

1 "Mae Foley, Famous Policewoman."

2 Scelfo, *Women Who Made New York*, 148.

3 "History of Women in the NYPD."

4 Scelfo, *Women Who Made New York*, 148.

5 Scelfo, *Women Who Made New York*, 148.

6 Scelfo, *Women Who Made New York*, 149.

7 "Wives of Police Protest Women in Patrol Cars," *New York Times*, June 21, 1974, https://www.nytimes.com/1974/06/21/archives/wives-of-police-protest-women-in-patrol-cars-action-endorsed.html.

8 Bartlett, "Famous Policewoman."

9 "Cruises Added to Honduras," *Brooklyn Daily Eagle*, March 23, 1942, https://bklyn.newspapers.com/image/52618382/?clipping_id=14012144.

10 "Cruises Added to Honduras."

11 Bren, *Barbizon*, 73.

Chapter 14. Déjà Vu

1 Maureen Callahan, "Victory Was Ours! NYC Hailed VE Day 75 Years Ago," *New York Post*, May 7, 2020, https://nypost.com/2020/05/07/nyc-hailed-v-e-day-75-years-ago/.

2   Duffin, *History in Blue*, 97.

3   Duffin, *History in Blue*, 97.

4   Bren, *Barbizon*, 84.

5   Norman Brouwer, "Defending New York City's Eastern Gateway: A History of Fort Totten on Willets Point," Bayside Historical Society, September 6, 2016, https://web.archive.org/web/20160906012609/http://www.hoflink.com/~bayside/brouwer.html.

6   Jen Carlson, "Flashback: NYC's War Time Dimouts," Gothamist, June 13, 2011, https://gothamist.com/arts-entertainment/flashback-nycs-war-time-dimouts

7   John Strausbaugh, *Victory City: A History of New York and New Yorkers During World War II* (New York: Hachette Book Group, 2018). 269–270.

8   "Thomas Dewey."

9   Zachary Keck, "World War II: Did the Nazis Sabotage a Ship in New York?," Center for the National Interest, November 15, 2020, https://nationalinterest.org/blog/reboot/world-war-ii-did-nazis-sabotage-ship-new-york-172574.

10   Bill O'Reilly and Martin Dugard, *Killing the Mob: The Fight Against Organized Crime in America* (New York: St. Martin's Press, 2021), 76–88.

11   Bill Sanderson, "How Nazi Spies Landed in the Hamptons for Secret Mission," *New York Post*, January 11, 2016, https://nypost.com/2016/06/11/how-nazi-spies-landed-in-the-hamptons-for-secret-mission/.

12   "Nazi Saboteurs and George Dasch," FBI History, accessed September 30, 2022, https://www.fbi.gov/history/famous-cases/nazi-saboteurs-and-george-dasch.

13   "Part V: Life During Wartime… From Nazi Spies to Bigamous Brides," FBI Commemorative World War II History television series, Sep 28, 2005. https://archives.fbi.gov/archives/news/stories/2005/september/history_092805.

14   "Long Island Hosted Nazi Spies in World War II," *Metro Long Island*, April 5, 2011, https://www.metro.us/long-island-hosted-nazi-spies-in-wwii/.

15   "Brooklyn Visitors Are Active in Social Life at Palm Beach," *Brooklyn Daily Eagle*, March 4, 1928, https://bklyn.newspapers.com/image/57569298/.

Chapter 15. Snowbird

1   Herb Mitgang, "VE Day New York," quoted in Robert Meyer Jr., ed., *The Stars and Stripes Story of World War II* (New York: David McKay, 1960), 446.

2   Sam Roberts, "New York 1945; The War Was Ending. Times Square Exploded. Change Was Coming," *New York Times*, July 30, 1995, https://www.nytimes.com/1995/07/30/nyregion/new-york-1945-the-war-was-ending-times-square-exploded-change-was-coming.html.

3   "VJ Day," National World War II Museum, accessed September 30, 2022, https://www.nationalww2museum.org/war/articles/v-j-day.

4   A. G. Sulzberger, "La Guardia's Tough and Incorruptible Police Commissioner," *New York Times*, November 11, 2009, https://archive.nytimes.com/cityroom .blogs.nytimes.com/2009/11/11/la-guardias-tough-and-incorruptible-police -commissioner/.

5   Janik, *Pistols and Petticoats*, 159.

6   "PPF History," New York City Police Pension Fund, accessed September 30, 2022, https://www1.nyc.gov/html/nycppf/html/home/home.shtml.

7   "35 Years on Force, Woman to Retire," *New York Times*, April 3, 1946, https://www .nytimes.com/1946/04/03/archives/35-years-on-force-woman-to-retire-mary -agnes-sullivan-has-been.html.

8   "Mae Foley, Famous Policewoman."

9   "Mae Foley, Famous Policewoman."

Chapter 16. Luck and Legacy

1   Bartlett, "Famous Policewoman."

2   Donald H. Thompson, *Lake Bomoseen: The Story of Vermont's Largest Little-Known Lake* (Charleston, SC: History Press, 2009), 36–40.

3   Ruff and Cronin, *New York City Police*, 83.

4   Duffin, *History in Blue*, 254.

5   "Efficient Policewoman Theresa Maria Melchionne," *New York Times*, October 29, 1963, https://www.nytimes.com/1963/10/29/archives/efficient-policewoman -theresa-maria-melchionne.html.

6   Theresa M. Melchionne, "Current Status and Problems of Women Police," *Journal of Criminal Law and Criminology* 58, no. 2 (1967): 257–60, https://scholarlycommons .law.northwestern.edu/cgi/viewcontent.cgi?article=5454&context=jclc.

7   "Who We Are," Police Benevolent Association of the City of New York, accessed September 30, 2022, http://nycpba.org/about-the-pba/who-we-are/.

8   "Pistol Packing Mama: Retired in Name Only," *Long Island City Star Journal*, November 17, 1957.

9   Aaron D. Backes, "Robert F. Wagner Jr.—History of New York City Mayors," Classic New York History, January 20, 2021, https://classicnewyorkhistory.com /robert-f-wagner-jr-history-of-new-york-city-mayors/.

10   "Pistol Packing Mama."

11   Piers Plowman and Stephen J. Card, *Queen of Bermuda and the Furness Bermuda Line* (Bermuda: Bermuda Maritime Press, 2002).

12   "History of Cruising," Cruise Jobs, November 6, 2012, https://cruise.jobs/history
      -of-cruising/.

13   Dennis Hevesi, "Frank D. O'Connor, 82, Is Dead," *New York Times*, December
      3, 1992, https://www.nytimes.com/1992/12/03/obituaries/frank-d-o-connor
      -82-is-dead-retired-new-york-appellate-judge.html.

14   Dennis Hevesi, "A Dynamo for Queens; John Thomas (Pat) Clancy," *New York
      Times*, January 6, 1959, https://www.nytimes.com/1959/01/06/archives/a--
      dynamo-for-queens-john-thomas-pat-clancy.html.

15   "Proclamation," Borough of Queens, City of New York, July 13, 1961.

16   "Pistol Packing Mama."

Chapter 17. A Legend Remembered

1   "Rev. Maurice Lenihan," *New York Times*, October 19, 1974, https://www.nytimes
      .com/1974/10/19/archives/rev-maurice-lenihan.html.

2   "Obituary for Mae Foley," New York *Daily News*, December 10, 1967.

3   Larry Celona and Linda Massarella, "Founding Member of NYPD Emerald Soci-
      ety Dies," *New York Post*, November 17, 2017, https://nypost.com/2017/11/19
      /founding-member-of-nypd-emerald-society-dies/

4   Pipes and Drums of the Emerald Society (website), accessed September 30,
      2022, https://nypdpipesanddrums.com/.

Chapter 18. Traditions and Progress

1   "Current NYPD Members of Service," NYC Civilian Complaint Review Board
      Data Transparency Initiative, accessed September 30, 2022, https://www1.nyc
      .gov/site/ccrb/policy/data-transparency-initiative-mos.page.

2   30x30 Initiative: Advancing Women in Policing (website), accessed September
      30, 2022, https://30x30initiative.org/.

3   "Women Police Officers called the Equal of Men," *New York Times*, June 11,
      1974, https://www.nytimes.com/1974/06/11/archives/women-police-officers
      -called-the-equal-of-men.html.

4   "Police Officer Irma Fran Lozada," Officer Down Memorial Page, accessed
      September 30, 2022, https://www.odmp.org/officer/8301-police-officer-irma
      -fran-lozada.

5   Peggy Noonan, "Why Crime Is Scarier Now," *Wall Street Journal*, July 7, 2022,
      https://www.wsj.com/articles/why-crime-scarier-policing-uvalde-elementary
      -highland-park-shootings-killed-11657228617.

6   Ivonne Roman, "How Policewomen Make Communities Safer," July 30, 2019,
     TED video, 5:43, https://www.ted.com/talks/ivonne_roman_how_policewomen
     _make_communities_safer.

7   Thomas S. Dee and Jaymes Pyne, "How to Get Cops Out of the Mental-Health
     Business," *Wall Street Journal*, July 8, 2022, https://www.wsj.com/articles/how
     -to-get-cops-out-of-the-mental-health-business-community-response-initiative
     -police-nonviolent-denver-social-workers-11657297784.

ABOUT THE AUTHOR

Mari K. Eder spent her first twenty years in the U.S. Army serving as a military police officer. While her experience in law enforcement in no way approximates the depth and breadth of experience of the true professional that Mae Foley was, she does have an appreciation for the challenges women have faced in challenging the brass ceiling and a deep respect for their accomplishments.